SUNSTRUCK

SUNSTRUCK

JAY ALLEN

Published in Australia and New Zealand in 2026
by Hachette Australia
(an imprint of Hachette Australia Pty Limited)
Gadigal Country, Level 17, 207 Kent Street, Sydney, NSW 2000
www.hachette.com.au

Hachette Australia acknowledges and pays our respects to the past and present Traditional Owners and Custodians of Country throughout Australia, and recognises the continuation of cultural, spiritual and educational practices of Aboriginal and Torres Strait Islander peoples. Our head office is located on the lands of the Gadigal people of the Eora Nation.

 A catalogue record for this book is available from the National Library of Australia

The authorised representative in the EEA is Hachette Ireland, 8 Castlecourt Centre, Dublin 15, D15 XTP3, Ireland (email: info@hbgi.ie).

ISBN: 978 0 7336 5328 5 (paperback)

Cover design by Alex Ross
Front cover photograph (author) courtesy of Jak Rowland
Cover photograph (beach) courtesy of Alamy/sammybez
Author photograph (right) on page 258 courtesy of Jenna Payn Photography
Typeset in 13/20.1 pt Minion Pro by Bookhouse, Sydney
Printed and bound in Australia by McPherson's Printing Group

The paper this book is printed on is certified against the Forest Stewardship Council® Standards. McPherson's Printing Group holds FSC® chain of custody certification SA-COC-005379. FSC® promotes environmentally responsible, socially beneficial and economically viable management of the world's forests.

To my family, and to everyone who has guided, encouraged and stood by me along my journey.

To those whose lives have been touched by melanoma or non-melanoma skin cancer, and to the families and friends of those we've lost – your strength inspires this work. May the Skin Check Trucks continue to bring hope and life-saving awareness to communities everywhere.

CONTENTS

PROLOGUE

Shit, I thought.

'Shit,' I said.

Looking back, it was a logical reaction, but in all honesty, in that moment I didn't really understand how bad the news was.

My GP had just called me. 'The results have come back. It's melanoma,' he said. 'You need to see a specialist immediately.' Back then, I didn't know enough to panic. I just thought, *Okay, they'll just cut it out, and we'll move on.* It sounded concerning, sure, but I figured it was fixable.

At the time, melanoma was just a word to me. I had no idea it was about to become my entire world.

We had people at our place for a barbecue when the doctor called, but he said to come in straight away, so we did. Leaving our guests to turn the snags, my partner, Janine, and I drove straight to the doctor's office. He sat us down and laid it all out. He'd been my GP since we moved to Ambarvale when I was eleven, but his manner was different that afternoon. Usually, he's calm and composed, but that day he seemed worried, a little panicked almost, which made me uneasy.

'Jay, this is serious,' he told me. 'You should have come to me earlier. Lucky we're acting now, because if we weren't . . .' He didn't need to finish the sentence.

It was clear it was bad, but I still wasn't especially worried. I just nodded along, agreeing to everything he said. When we got back in the car, I still wasn't overly fazed. 'Alright,' I said. 'They'll sort it out, and we'll get on with things.'

Janine's optimism also kept me from worrying. She's such a positive person, always looking on the bright side, and that helped. I was super calm in that moment – just took the news in my stride, as if it were just another errand to handle. Later, as I started to wrap my head around everything, the seriousness of the situation would start to sink in. But in that moment, I was just a bloke with a mole that had been removed, not someone staring down a life-threatening diagnosis.

The mole I'd had removed had never caused me any pain. To be honest, I thought it was just a blister caused by my work boots rubbing against my left ankle. I'd take my socks off after a long shift and notice blood on them, but even then, I didn't think it was serious. The mole was about the size of a five-cent piece – a bit too big to ignore completely, but not alarming enough to think it was cancer. The thing was, it just wouldn't heal.

I developed a habit of scratching it constantly. My fingers would automatically go to it. After a while, the irritation felt almost normal. I brushed it off, figuring it would sort itself out. Cancer wasn't even a thought in my mind during those days.

The last couple of months before the mole was removed, though, something changed. I remember this one night vividly. It was just after midnight, and I was getting ready for my early-morning shift at work. I went into the bathroom, and I just felt . . . off. It was like I had an itch I couldn't scratch, but it wasn't *on* my skin, it was underneath it. It started happening more often. I'd get this weird restless feeling in the middle of the night, and I had no idea why. Looking back, I think my body was trying to tell me something wasn't right.

In my first specialist appointment with Doctor Michael Quinn, a couple of weeks after I got the call from the GP, I mentioned this sensation to him. 'It was probably your immune system fighting off the cancer,' he explained. That stopped me in my tracks. That whole time, my body had been battling cancer, and I'd had no idea.

He told me melanoma can trigger the immune system to react in unusual ways. 'Your body was probably working overtime trying to fight off the cancer cells,' he said. 'That's the best explanation I can give for what you were feeling.'

On the one hand, it was a relief to know that my body had been fighting for me. On the other, it was terrifying to think how close I had come to ignoring the signs entirely. Looking back, that uneasy feeling in the middle of the night might have been one of the few things that saved me.

It was a lot to process. Up to that point, I'd never had any major health issues. Sure, I'd broken my collarbone playing footy and had my nose broken a few times, the usual rough-and-tumble stuff. But nothing like this. I was tanned, fit and had just proposed to the love of my life. I didn't know anyone else my age who'd been through something like this.

Doctor Quinn explained how easily melanoma could spread, and how quickly it could become life-threatening. But even then, I was still in denial, treating this as something to tick off a list instead of a crisis I had to tackle head-on.

When he asked if I could think of anything that might have caused the melanoma, I mentioned that I regularly used solariums. He was intrigued. 'How often have you used them?' he asked.

I paused for a moment, doing the maths in my head before replying, 'Maybe forty or fifty times? And some of those were double sessions.'

He nodded. 'That could very well be a significant factor here.'

I found myself reflecting on all those times I had jumped into a solarium without a second thought, chasing a tan. It was a sobering realisation.

Still, I walked out of his office thinking it was manageable. 'It'll all be fine,' I reassured myself.

It wasn't until we were driving home from the city that it really hit me. This wasn't just a mole. This wasn't something that could just be cut out and forgotten about. This was serious.

I had always thought cancer was a disease for someone else, someone older and further along in life.

I was about to learn the harsh truth: that melanoma was the most common cancer in young Australians aged twenty to thirty-nine. Not one of the most common. *The* most common. At thirty-two years old, I was right in that age bracket, and like most people my age, I thought I was bulletproof.

But the stats were shocking, and suddenly terrifyingly real. I remembered reading that someone in Australia dies from melanoma every six hours. That means while you're watching a footy match, someone loses their life to this thing. And I bet they didn't think it would happen to them, either.

All those years chasing the perfect tan, trying to look good, I wasn't just rolling the dice. I was stacking them against myself. I later learned that using a solarium before the age of thirty-five increased your risk of melanoma by seventy-five per cent. But back then, no-one was talking about that. There were no warnings, no signs saying, *This could kill you.* Just palm trees on the walls and the smell of coconut oil.

That call from the GP would come to define me for life. From then on, I was no longer simply Jay Allen. I was The Melanoma Man.

1

ELBOWS OFF THE TABLE

Much like sun safety, I was barely a thought in the early 1970s. The hole in the ozone layer was decades off becoming dinner table conversation, and in Australia, the land of endless beaches and backyard barbies, the outdoors was king. A deep tan wasn't just fashionable; it was necessary, a badge of honour. Healthy, sexy, a sign you were living life right. Everybody wanted that golden glow.

For my dad, John Allen, that bronzed Aussie lifestyle was just part of the deal. Dad had grown up in the Illawarra, south of Sydney, until he was sixteen years old, when he moved to Parramatta, in Sydney's western suburbs. Dad was carefree as they come – his world revolved around sun, surf and his mates.

But life was different for my mum, Julie, who grew up fair-skinned and red-haired in Parramatta. Mum was the quiet achiever in her family, known for her work ethic and her no-nonsense attitude. She started work in a dress shop at fourteen and nine months, determined to make her way in life. Her fiery red hair might've set her apart, but it was her determination that defined her. She was just thirteen when she met my dad, who was sixteen. They went to the same school, and lived two houses away from each other.

It was a short courtship. By the time Mum was sixteen, they were married, and Fiona, my older sister, came along soon after. Two years later, in 1975, I turned up. I got Mum's fair complexion and fiery red hair – a stark contrast to Dad's and Fiona's olive skin.

We grew up in a tiny Housing Commission home in Airds, in Campbelltown. It was snug, to say the least, but it was home. That three-bedroom house held everything that mattered. The lounge room was the heart of the home. Beyond that was the kitchen, and then the bedrooms, all in a neat row. Mum and Dad's was on the right, mine in the middle and Fiona's on the left.

The backyard was small, just a patch of grass and a shed, but to us kids, it was a kingdom. Dad built a timber pergola out the front, and a little garden wrapped around it. There was a laneway next to our house and a court-yard at the back, which became our makeshift footy field. We'd spend hours there, booting the ball around with the neighbours' kids. Endless games of backyard footy, scraped knees and arguments over whether the goalposts were 'just there' or 'a bit more to the left'.

Those afternoons might not sound like much, but they were everything to us – just simple joys. When the sun started setting and Mum called us in for dinner, we'd drag ourselves inside, sweaty and covered in dirt, but smiling. Those days were good – simple, but perfect.

Two years after I came along, Mum gave birth to her third child, Shauna. Shauna had the same fiery red hair as me – *the trademark Cullen colouring*, Mum would say. But Shauna's story was heartbreakingly short. She was born premature, and there was nothing they could do to save her – back then, medical technology wasn't as good as it is today. Shauna only lived for five days. The loss hit my parents hard, and we lived under a cloud of grief for a long time.

After losing Shauna, Mum and Dad worked tirelessly to keep our family afloat, doing everything they could to shield us from life's harsh realities. Times were tough, but they made sure we always had what we needed.

And life carried on, as it does. I kept playing footy in the laneway. Dad kept building stuff and tinkering around the house. And somehow, Mum kept everything running smoothly. Slowly, laughter returned to our family, though there was always a little piece missing. Those years in Airds were so simple, so small, but they gave me roots, a sense of where I came from. And, most of all, they taught me how to keep going, no matter what life hands you.

•

At home, Mum and Dad ran a tight ship. From the moment we were old enough to hold a broom or set the table, we had jobs to do. My folks believed in teaching responsibility early, and we were all expected to pitch in – it was a team effort. Above all, the thing they were strictest about was the importance of good manners, especially at mealtimes. There was no eating with your mouth open, no elbows on the table, and we always sat down as a family to eat dinner together. Those moments around the table, swapping stories about our day, are some of my best memories. We laughed, talked and sometimes argued, but it was always together.

Mum made sure we were well fed. She was, and still is, a brilliant cook. She made sure we had vegetables with every meal, whether it was a simple pork chop or a roast.

Takeaway was a rare treat, saved for special occasions. When we did have it, it felt like Christmas had come early. I remember those days when Mum would give me $3 or $4 to head to the Airds shops. Back then, you could get a big bag of hot chips, wrapped in white paper, steaming and doused in barbecue sauce. It was simple, but we thought it was the best thing ever. Those chips were the height of indulgence for us kids.

Most of the time, though, it was sandwiches, fruit and whatever Mum whipped up at home. For lunch, we used to buy stuff from the school canteen that came in a brown paper bag. Every Sunday, without fail, Mum would make a baked dinner. Roast meat, veggies, gravy, the works. She still does it to this day, and it's just as good as I remember. Mum always made sure we ate well, breakfast, lunch and dinner. She wasn't one to cut corners when it came to food, no matter how tight things were.

Weekends were always a bit of a production in the kitchen. Mum would cook a big breakfast on Saturdays or Sundays – fry-ups with eggs, bacon, toast, the lot. Lunch would follow, then a proper dinner in the evening. Even now, Mum's still the same, making sure Dad's got sandwiches for work and that everyone's fed. She took pride in keeping us healthy and happy.

Holidays were modest but memorable. We'd pack up and head down the coast to Bulli, where my grandmother lived, as well as my aunty Janet and uncle Brian and all my cousins. It wasn't far, but it felt like a proper getaway. We'd spend the day with family, eat until we were stuffed and play endless games of footy. Dad's mum had a big shed out the back with a pool table, so we'd take on the cousins for a few games, then jump on our bikes and ride around the Bulli racetrack or down to the beach.

When we weren't holidaying in Bulli, we'd go to Coledale, further up the coast. My pop had a house there, right up on the clifftops. It was the kind of place you see on postcards, with beautiful views of the ocean. You could hear the waves crashing below. We'd spend the morning watching little penguins waddle along the shore, then get straight into a day of sun, sand and surf. It was pure magic.

Mum and Dad weren't religious, but they valued respect and discipline. That was how they'd been raised, and they were the same with us. If you did something wrong, you knew you were in for it. Sometimes, just the thought of Dad finding out was enough to keep us in line. We still squabbled, though, like all siblings do. We bickered about the silliest things, like who got the biggest slice of cake, who had to do the dishes or who started it. Most of the time, it was harmless, but every now and then, we crossed the line.

One time, I threw a cup at Fiona. I can't remember why – probably just in a fit of rage. The cup hit her square on the back of the head, and she needed stitches. It's easily the most aggressive thing I've ever done and boy, did I pay for it. That night, when Dad got home, I got the telling-off of my life, and I was grounded for three weeks. I certainly never threw another cup, and I kept my elbows off the table for a good while after that.

Dad's go-to punishment was grounding. We'd spend a stint in our room, locked away from the rest of the house and the outside world. In the heat of the moment, Dad would often ground us for a month, swearing he wouldn't change his mind, but he was soft at heart. A week or so in, he'd usually come around and let us off early. Still, those weeks felt like a lifetime. Coming home from school, knowing you'd be stuck in your room with no TV, no toys and, worst of all, no outside play. It was brutal. But it worked. We learned our lesson.

Despite the strict rules and occasional punishments, our childhood in Airds was full of joy. Living on a Housing Commission estate, we were part of a close-knit community – everyone knew everyone else. The kids in the neighbourhood were always around, and we never strayed too far from home. We played footy in the laneway, rode our bikes, or just mucked around until the streetlights flicked on and Mum called us in for dinner. It wasn't fancy, but it was a good childhood – lots of laughter and a sense of belonging.

As kids, our lives revolved around the outdoors, no matter the season or weather. The moment the sun came up, we'd grab our footies, cricket bats and bikes, and race out the door. The streets of the housing estate were like our playground, and we had endless adventures. We'd spend hours outside, playing cricket in the street, riding our bikes, kicking the footy barefoot on the road.

Back then, sun safety wasn't really a thing. Sunscreen? Never heard of it. Hats? No chance. If you got burnt, you got burnt. Peeling sunburnt skin off each other's backs was like a gross competition to see who could get the longest strip of skin. Getting burnt was just part of life, like scraped knees or stubbed toes. It was normal. We were years off learning to slip, slop, slap. Skin cancer never even crossed our minds – to us, cancer was some distant disease that only happened to really old people. It wasn't on our radar at all.

When we weren't outside, I had my own little routine. I loved watching *CHiPs*, a show about two motorbike cops.

Every afternoon, I'd be glued to the TV. After *CHiPs*, I'd switch over to *Skippy the Bush Kangaroo*. Those two shows were my staples. Once they were over, I'd either head to footy training or be out playing with my mates until the sun went down. And, of course, there was Rugby League on TV. I'd watch it religiously, whether it was a big game or just highlights. Footy was always on my mind, whether I was playing it, watching it or dreaming about where it might take me.

At school, my world didn't expand much beyond the familiar streets of Airds. My first school was John Warby Public School, just 300 metres from our house. I already knew most of the kids there. The mates I'd spent my days kicking the footy with were the same ones I found myself sharing a desk with.

I'd like to think I was one of the popular kids at school – I was a bit of a chatterbox who got along with everyone. Academically, I wasn't too bad. I gave it a good crack, mostly because I was worried about getting a bad report and disappointing my parents. Even so, every single one of my reports said the same thing: 'easily distracted', 'talks too much'. They weren't wrong. Socialising was my strength, but it was also my weakness. Still, the fear of report card day was enough to keep me on my toes . . . most of the time.

There was one time I really crossed the line, though. In Year 6, we went on a four-day school camp. On the very first day, for some reason, I decided to throw a potato at one of the teachers. It nailed her on the back of the head – turns out I'm pretty good at headshots. Luckily, it didn't do much damage other than leaving bits of potato in her hair, but still, they weren't happy. I got sent straight home.

I would've been grounded and stuck inside my room for months if Dad had found out, but I got lucky – he was at work when the school called. Instead, they got Mum. I'm not sure how I managed it, but somehow I talked her into hiding me under my bunk bed for the next three days so Dad wouldn't find out I'd been sent home.

When I was eight, Mum announced she was pregnant again, with another baby girl. Chantal, with her sunny smile and cheeky laugh, brought a whole new dynamic to our family. Mum adored her, and even Dad, who wasn't the most sentimental bloke, was like a marshmallow around her. Chantal quickly became the golden child, doted on and spoiled. But we didn't mind. She fit seamlessly into our family, lighting up the room with her infectious energy.

By this time, Mum and Dad were working harder than ever. Dad, who had been working as a coalminer, had ditched the mines and taken up truck driving, a job that kept him busy around the clock. He was rarely home, but when he was, he made the time count. Mum, meanwhile, juggled everything else – household chores, raising three kids and taking on extra paid work wherever she could. I've got no doubt the juggle was hard on my parents – even as kids, we knew how much they were sacrificing – but they were determined. They were building something better for us.

When I was eleven, everything changed – Mum and Dad bought their own place. They'd scrimped and saved for years, and finally, they had enough to put down for a house-and-land package. It was a massive deal, a huge leap from our little Housing Commission place to something they could call their own. This was their dream, what they'd been working toward all these years, over all those late nights and long shifts.

The new house was a bit bigger: it had four bedrooms and a proper backyard. It still wasn't much by most people's standards, but to us, it was everything. That home was full of happiness – birthdays, Christmases and countless lazy afternoons. It was where Chantal grew into the charming, cheeky kid she was destined to be. It became the place that would anchor us for the rest of our lives.

Buying the house was a bit of a turning point for us, thanks to all of Mum and Dad's hard work. They never slowed down, though. Mum ran the house like clockwork while Dad was out on the road, driving trucks to make ends meet. Meanwhile, I threw myself into school and footy – mostly footy, if I'm being completely honest. From as far back as I can remember, football was my life. My dream was to make it to the NRL, and I went after it hard. Dad was a hundred per cent on board, driving me to training, cheering me on.

It was also around this time that I discovered girls. My first crush was a girl called Samantha, a tall blonde who joined our school in Year 6. We 'dated' in the way eleven-year-olds do, which is to say we probably held hands once.

But Samantha wasn't my first love.

That honour belonged to footy.

2

BRONZED AMBITION

From the moment I picked up a footy at the age of five, I was hooked. Footy was everything to me. It shaped my childhood and defined me as I grew up. I dreamed of making it to the NRL, and I was hell-bent on making it happen.

My obsession went far beyond the footy oval. I didn't just want to play the game, I wanted to know everything about it. Dad used to bring home two magazines every week: *Big League* and *Rugby League Week*. *Big League* was packed with player stats and all the upcoming fixtures. *Rugby League Week* had more in-depth articles and behind-the-scenes stories. I'd hang out for each new issue. *Rugby League Week* usually came out on a Wednesday, while *Big League* dropped on a Thursday, giving me a double dose each week. I'd stack them under my bed like treasure, reading them over and over.

I started playing for the Campbelltown Warriors when I was five, and I often played in higher age groups. The ball was almost as big as I was back then. I kept at it, season after season, all through my junior years. By the time I hit high school, Rugby League was pretty much my life. I had two training sessions a week, and games every Saturday morning. Sundays were reserved for watching the A-grade and reserve grade matches with my dad.

Basically, my weeks revolved around footy. Dad was just as involved as I was. He coached my team at times, as well as other teams. When I wasn't at my own training sessions, I'd tag along to Dad's. Playing footy seven days a week was just normal for us.

While Rugby League consumed most of my life, I did have one other hobby, although it was still related to footy: commentating. I wasn't really into music, and so, while all my mates were busy learning the chords to AC/DC songs, I used my trusty radio and tape recorder to tune into live broadcasts of games. I'd grab the latest issue of

Big League, head to my room, lay out the stats and start recording, pretending I was live on air.

'This is Jay from 2GB,' I'd announce in my most professional voice. 'It's Canterbury versus Parramatta, and Sterling passes to Kenny. Kenny's in the corner! What a try!' I'd keep going until Mum called me for dinner. Those afternoons were pure happiness for me, the perfect outlet for my passion.

Starting at Airds High School wasn't a huge change, but it felt significant. The school was only a kilometre away from John Warby Public School, but that short walk across the ovals was like entering a different world. In those days, the area around the school was mostly bushland, a bit wild and rugged, which made the walk to school feel like a kind of adventure. It was a simpler time, when kids played outside and screen time was a rare treat, not something we spent all day doing.

High school was a blur of mates, footy and staying out of trouble. I didn't have any enemies, which is probably why I enjoyed those years so much – honestly, they were some of the best of my life.

Not surprisingly, my favourite subject was physical education. PE was the subject where I could really shine, though I did okay in most subjects. I got on pretty well with the teachers, which helped, especially in subjects like English, science and woodwork. Those subjects felt rewarding. Maths, on the other hand, was a different story. Numbers and I just didn't get along – that's something that never changed.

I had plenty of fun with my mates, too. We'd meet up at the local fair, walk around holding hands with our girlfriends and sneak in a few stolen kisses. Nothing serious, just casual crushes that usually fizzled out pretty quickly. After school, we'd skate around the neighbourhood or play footy, usually coming home bruised and bleeding but pretty happy.

When I was fourteen, I got my first job, at McDonald's. I threw myself into it despite the ungodly hours. I'd ride my skateboard from Ambarvale, up and down the steep hills to the Campbelltown McDonald's, ready for a 4 am shift. Years later, Mum would still talk about those early morning starts – honestly, I think she was amazed I managed to get there on time. I worked the front counter, flipped burgers and sometimes snuck free food to my mates. It was my first taste of independence – finally, I was earning my own money and learning the value of hard work, something my parents had been demonstrating my whole life.

I spent a good chunk of my earnings on Matchbox cars. I had a growing collection, and Mum would surprise me with a new one whenever she could. Christmas mornings were the best, unwrapping these amazing service station sets and racing my cars around imaginary tracks.

Of course, being a kid, I was constantly getting into mischief. One time, my cousin and I decided to test out a lighter on Mum's fern in the lounge room. Before we knew it, the whole thing went up in flames. We scrambled to put it out, but the fire left scorch marks on the ceiling, which we desperately tried to scrub off before my parents got home. Luckily, they didn't go too hard on us, probably because it had been my cousin's idea.

My grandparents were a big part of my childhood, too. Mum's dad passed away from a brain tumour when I was around fourteen. I remember visiting him in hospital, sitting there in that sterile room, watching this strong man fade away. Dad's dad had cancer as well, and we'd visit him at the Royal Prince Alfred Hospital (RPA). But even then, it didn't register how dangerous cancer was. I still saw it as something that happened to old people. Not me. Not my mates.

At that age, cancer felt like something that happened to other people. It wasn't something boys my age talked about. We were young, invincible, more worried about whether our biceps looked good or if we'd get picked for the rep side. Even seeing my grandparents suffer, it still didn't land. I just thought: that's what happens when you get old. Not in a million years would I have thought that, years later, I'd be back there at RPA myself, going through the same thing.

•

As I got more and more serious about football, I started going to the gym, too. It started with basic weights sessions, trying to bulk up for footy, just a few machines at the local rec centre. But by the late eighties, commercial gyms were more mainstream, and before long, the gym was like my second home. My footy club started pushing strength and conditioning more seriously, so I'd be in there most afternoons, pushing iron, learning new exercises and sizing myself up in the mirrors.

There was a culture to it – radio blasting in the background, protein shakes between sets, guys spotting each other while talking. It seemed like everyone was training for something, even if it was just to look the part. And by then, most gyms had a solarium – a little room with a stand-up tube or a lie-down bed, glowing with an eerie blue light.

It wasn't really something my mates and I were into. We were there to train, not to tan. But I definitely noticed the shift. Solariums were for the guys who wanted to look ripped and tanned, the full package. You'd see bodybuilders, tradies and even a few footy players using them. Looking good was starting to matter just as much as playing good.

By the middle of high school, I was playing in the Harold Matthews Cup for the Under-15s, which was a big deal. I'd fought hard to get a spot on that team. Invitations were sent to the players who were considered good enough to try out. But I didn't get one. I was crushed. Footy was my life – it was everything to me – so not being invited felt like a slap in the face. To make matters worse, a mate of mine whose dad was well connected in the league did get a letter – and boy, did he enjoy rubbing my face in it. 'You didn't get a letter,' he'd say mockingly in front of our school mates. It stung and, I'll admit, it dampened my spirits.

But life has a funny way of levelling the playing field. The initial tryouts came and went, and it turned out the selectors weren't satisfied with the talent pool. They announced a second round of open trials, inviting anyone to have a go. My dad wasn't going to let me miss this opportunity. 'We're going,' he said. And so we did.

That second trial changed everything. I poured my heart into it, determined to prove myself. And when the selections were announced, I'd made the squad. Meanwhile, my mate, the guy who had teased me about not getting an invitation? He didn't make the cut. I have to say, that felt kind of poetic. It wasn't just about getting on the team; it was about showing that hard work and persistence could win out over privilege and connections.

In high school, parties were a regular thing, and there'd always be someone offering a drink or a smoke. Drugs started creeping in, too. I'd see it all happening around me, but it was never my thing. I would have footy the next day, and that was all the reason I needed. There was no way I was going to mess around with anything that would affect how well I played. My focus was on footy, and there was no room for distractions.

For me, it was both about avoiding trouble and about staying committed. My footy training meant everything to me. Go to school, train, sleep, repeat – that was my life. While my mates were getting caught up in partying, I was leaving it all on the field. It was football, football, football, and I wouldn't have had it any other way.

I did find time for one other focus, though: girls. In Year 9, I started going out with my first long-term girlfriend, a girl in the year below, and I was hooked. When I finished Year 12, I did something I never thought I'd do – I repeated the year so I could stay in her year group. Crazy, right? But young love does strange things to a person, and at the time, it felt like the most logical decision in the world.

My girlfriend was the best-looking girl in the school, and our relationship was a bit of a roller-coaster. She'd break up with me, go out with someone else, and I'd be crushed. Then she'd come back, and I'd take her back without hesitation. I lost count of how many times this cycle repeated itself. Even so, she was a huge part of my life, and my family adored her as well. Mum and Dad would lend her the family car, and she became almost like a third daughter to them. It wasn't just a teenage romance; it was more serious than that.

My high school years were bliss, mostly, but it wasn't all smooth sailing.

When I was about thirteen, my dad had a big truck accident. It's still one of the most traumatic memories of my childhood. It happened just after we'd moved into our new house. Life was already a juggle back then, with Mum and Dad working flat out to stay afloat, and Dad's accident threw everything into chaos.

He was out at Concord, working on his truck, as he often did. Dad was the kind of bloke who'd take care of his own repairs – it saved a bit of money, and honestly, he enjoyed the work. Trucks were his world, his livelihood and his passion, too. On this day, he was working underneath the truck, doing some kind of repair, with a brick chocked behind the wheel to stop the truck from rolling.

When he loosened the tail shaft, the whole truck started to move – the brick didn't hold. The truck rolled right over it, picking up speed as it went down the hill. Dad, still underneath, had no time to react. As the truck rolled, the tail shaft spun violently, slamming into his head. The force was enough to fracture his skull and cause bleeding on the brain. The truck finally came to a stop when it smashed into a parked car further down the hill.

But the damage had already been done.

3
DARK CLOUDS

Dad was rushed to the hospital, where he stayed for about eight weeks. The doctors weren't sure he'd make it. Mum was beside herself, trying to hold it all together for us kids while grappling with the possibility of losing him. It was a tough time. We'd visit him regularly, and seeing him hooked up to machines, bandaged and fighting for his life was tough for a thirteen-year-old to process.

And when he finally came home, that wasn't the end of the ordeal. He couldn't work for about twelve months, which put a massive strain on our family. To make matters worse, Dad had missed a monthly payment on his insurance, so there was no payout to help us keep our heads above water. Amazingly, other people, including the company Dad contracted for, helped out financially. It was very kind.

I don't know how Mum and Dad managed to get through it. That whole experience just proved their resilience and determination to keep going, no matter what life threw at them. Dad eventually recovered and got back to work, but the incident had a lasting impact on all of us. It was a stark reminder of how quickly life could change, and how fragile even the toughest blokes could be.

Living in a tight-knit community, tragedy would hit us like a tidal wave. When something terrible happened, it wasn't just something that happened to someone else, a juicy bit of gossip whispered over fences – it affected all of us.

When I was fourteen, a guy in our town committed murder. His name was Clint, and he lived at the top of our street with his blue cattle dog. Clint wasn't old, probably only eighteen or nineteen, but when you're still in high school, anyone who's finished school seems like an adult. He had this air about him that screamed trouble, and he knew it. He'd set his dog on us kids just to watch us panic, laughing as we sprinted away. It was clear he liked being feared.

One afternoon, I was at a mate's house in Ambarvale, about six or seven kilometres from Airds, when the house phone rang. My mate answered it and said it was for me, which was a bit unusual. The fact that it was my mum on the line immediately set off alarm bells.

'Stay there. Stay inside,' she told me. 'Clint from up the road is on the run from the police. He . . . he chopped up his girlfriend with a machete.'

I froze. Clint had always been a scary guy, but this? I couldn't wrap my mind around it. His girlfriend was quiet and polite, and I'd often see her walking his dog. She was the total opposite of this bloke we all knew to avoid. And now, she was gone. Brutally murdered.

Clint didn't get far. The coppers caught him not long after, but he didn't stick around to face justice. That night, in the Campbelltown cells, he took his own life. It was a swift, grim end to a horrifying chapter, and the events left our community shaken to the core. The street didn't feel safe anymore.

Not long after that, tragedy struck again. A lovely woman lived in the house across the road from Clint's place with her young children. They were a beautiful family, regulars at street barbecues and Christmas get-togethers. The mum always had a big smile, and her kids were full of energy, running around and laughing. Then one night, their house caught fire.

Back then, not all houses had smoke detectors like they do now, so there was no warning, no alarm. The fire moved fast, and the family didn't make it out. This street that had once been so full of life suddenly felt empty. We were still raw from what had happened with Clint, and now this. The sadness and shock was just so heavy.

A few days later, I wandered over to the charred remains of their house. I don't know why – maybe I was drawn by morbid curiosity, or maybe I was just trying to make sense of it all. As I sifted through the rubble, I spotted a photograph lying in the ash. It was a picture of the family, smiling and happy. I picked it up, and for the first time, the weight of everything hit me like a punch to the gut.

These weren't just headlines or stories you hear about people you've never met. They were real people – our neighbours, our friends – and now they were gone. I stood there clutching that photo, feeling like my heart was breaking.

It took a long time for the community to even begin healing after those tragedies. The losses left a hole that couldn't be easily filled. But, being a close-knit community, people pulled together. It was like everyone understood that life had to go on, even if it wasn't the same.

And eventually, things did start to feel a bit lighter. Kids got back to playing in the streets, neighbours began hosting barbecues again. It seemed like everyone understood they needed to move forward. We didn't forget what had happened, but we knew we had to keep going.

Then, just as the cracks were starting to mend, tragedy struck once more. This time, I was the one who did the damage. I hit a mate from school with my car.

●

I can still see his face. He was lying there on the ground not moving, his mouth open, and I honestly thought he was going to die. The memory is burnt into my brain. The wait for the cops and ambos to arrive felt like it took forever.

Our neighbourhood came alive the moment they heard the crash. People poured out of their houses, crowding the street, desperate to find out what had happened and who was responsible. And right there, in the middle of the chaos, was my banged-up Pizza Hut delivery car.

I was seventeen at the time, delivering pizzas for a bit of extra cash. It had been an ordinary shift when, out of nowhere, he appeared on his bike, riding straight out in front of my car. I didn't even have time to react. To make matters worse, he was coming from my ex-girlfriend's house. Talk about rubbing salt into the wound.

Sitting there waiting for the ambos, I kept thinking, *This can't be real. This can't actually be happening.* The guilt was massive, and totally overwhelming, even though I knew it wasn't my fault. I knew I hadn't been speeding – I'd slowed down to check the house number for the delivery – but that didn't change what had happened, or how awful I felt. He was only sixteen, and he'd pulled out in front of me without looking. It was all just a tragic mistake.

And he wasn't just any kid. He was a brilliant swimmer, the kind of kid who scooped up awards like it was nothing, and everyone expected big things from him. The accident changed all that in an instant. Going back to school after it happened was one of the hardest things I've ever had to do. Word spread fast, of course, as we were a tight-knit community, and naturally, people started taking sides. Some blamed me – not everyone, but still, it felt like everyone was watching me.

The whole thing was really stressful – for me and for my mate who was injured. The case ended up in court as part of the insurance claim, and the prosecution tried to argue that I'd been speeding, claiming I'd been doing seventy-eight or eighty in a seventy zone. They went all out, too – they brought in cars to recreate the scenario, took measurements and basically did everything they could to make it seem like I'd been reckless. But the truth was on my side – it was confirmed that their calculations didn't add up. As a result, my mate couldn't claim any compensation, which only added to the stress.

Pizza Hut gave me a month off work, but even when I went back, things weren't the same. The car was fixed, but the whispers and the stares didn't stop. Everyone knew about the accident, and no-one was going to let me forget.

I dreamed about the accident for months afterward. I'd see his face staring back at me, his tongue hanging out, and wake up drenched in sweat. The image haunted me.

All these tragedies – Dad's accident, Clint's murder, the fire and then the accident – were things I carried around with me for years afterward, well into adulthood. I didn't realise it at the time, but those experiences really shaped the way I dealt with trauma – or, more accurately, how I didn't deal with it. In my house, we didn't talk about our feelings. Sure, my parents made sure I was okay, but back in those days, if something bad happened, you got on with it. You went to school, had your dinner, kept your elbows off the table. That was just what we did. And so I learned to shove everything down deep and pretend I was fine.

I never talked to anyone about the accident, never saw a psychologist or got any help. I didn't talk to my mates. I didn't even tell Dad how much it was messing with my head. I just bottled it up and kept going, got back in the car and went back to work. The same thing happened years later, when I was diagnosed with melanoma. I heard the word 'cancer', and something in me just shut down. I nodded. I listened. And then I did what I'd always done – I kept it to myself. I didn't want to worry anyone. I didn't want to seem weak. I was that same little kid who'd seen all that tragedy. I just had a better poker face.

•

Footy provided the perfect distraction – it was exactly what I needed. In Years 11 and 12, I was captain of the school footy team. It was a massive responsibility, and I thrived on it. As captain, I got to pick the school team, working with the PE coach to decide who would make the cut. By then I was playing footy at a representative level, so I knew what to look for and how to strategise. I loved every moment of it.

After I left school, my dad lined up a bricklaying apprenticeship for me. He was always trying to set me up for a stable future. I gave it a go, but honestly, it was brutal. The work was relentless, stacking and laying bricks all day, and the physical toll was unlike anything I'd ever experienced. It wasn't just the hard work; it was the fact that I was doing the same thing, over and over again, all day long. I'd stand there, covered in dust, looking at the sky and praying for rain – anything to cut the day short.

To make matters worse, I'd spend the whole time worrying about my girlfriend, Jane. She was gorgeous, and that made me insecure. I wouldn't say I was overly possessive, but I did stress a lot about what she was up to while I was at work. I'd be on the job site, lugging bricks, and my mind would be racing with fears about what she might be doing.

I stuck it out for a few months, but I really couldn't take it anymore. My boss had promised me a company ute if I stayed on, but I couldn't do it. I'd often stand around, staring at the clouds, thinking, *This isn't what I want for my life.* Bricklaying is a tough gig, and I have total respect for anyone who can do it, but it just wasn't for me.

Meanwhile, I was still chasing my dream of making it big in Rugby League. I was training hard, playing harder, hell-bent on the chance to play professional footy.

I'd been a standout for the Appin Warriors for a few years, and was even named the club's highest point scorer and their best back. The next step seemed clear: Western Suburbs, a legendary NRL club, one of the oldest in New South Wales. They reached out, inviting me to join their Jersey Flegg team. I can still remember the thrill I felt when they bumped me up to the Presidents Cup squad to train the off-season, a level just shy of reserve grade. At eighteen, I was on the brink of first grade, living the dream and training alongside players who would go on to have amazing careers. Coach Billy Bowling saw potential in me as a halfback, and even hinted at making me captain.

But then, a twist. My dad read an article in the *Daily Telegraph* about an open trial day for the Cronulla Sharks, and he suggested I try out. It didn't make much sense since I was already doing well at Western Suburbs, but I trusted his judgement, so I went. I played the open trial and it ended up being one of my best games ever. The coach, Johnny Lang, and then CEO Shane Richardson took interest in me, coming down at half-time to ask me some questions. After the game, they invited me to train with the club for the off-season, saying they would consider me for a contract after a month. I was over the moon. During the off-season, I was training alongside the reserve grade and first grade. The Sharks' first-grade team was filled with stars like Andrew Ettingshausen and Mitch Healey, so I was a bit awe-struck. In the first session at Caltex Field in Cronulla, I remember being introduced to Paul Green, as we were both halfbacks. Paul had just come down from Queensland, and while I didn't know who he was then, he would later go on to play for Australia. He was a legend.

But even though I gave it my all during the tough pre-season training and the month-long trials, I didn't get a contract, and now I had nothing. I tried to return to Western Suburbs, but I'd blown my chance. The coach said they couldn't justify dropping players who'd stayed loyal to make room for me. It was devastating. I'd gone from being a rising star to being cut out entirely.

I was rapidly learning that, in life, things could change quickly, and you couldn't always rely on things going right. But I was also building resilience. I learned how to survive when things went pear-shaped. What I didn't know, however, was how to sit in my pain and face it. Instead, I just ran harder – on the field, in the gym, in relationships. I sprinted away from my emotions like they were chasing me down the sideline. Finally, when I couldn't outrun them anymore, they hit like a front-row forward.

4

TOO YOUNG TO KNOW, TOO STONED TO TRY

Football was my first love, and losing it felt like losing a part of myself. The dedication that had fuelled me through years of training and sacrifice faded, and I was left feeling lost and aimless. I'd always been a pretty driven person, but after my footy career fell apart, it was like all that drive just drained out of me. I stopped caring about the things that had been important to me. Instead of focusing on the future, what I wanted to do and where I wanted to end up, I drifted aimlessly, and ended up way off course.

The year after finishing Year 12 was a bit of a blur. Suddenly, the structure and routine of school were gone, and I was left staring at an open-ended question: what now? The days stretched out endlessly. I had no direction, and I was bored. Once I gave up the apprenticeship, I wasn't working, didn't have a clear path and just spent my time hanging around my mates in Airds. It was a recipe for trouble.

I was searching for something to fill the void, and that's when I found pot. It was my way of escaping. When you're stoned, the hours blur together, and the boredom doesn't sting as much. It's like hitting pause on reality. The trouble is, reality's still there when the high wears off.

My mates were my constant companions during that time. Some of them were friends from school, others from footy, and some just from around Airds. We were a tight group, and most of us had the same sense of aimlessness. I'd often see my mates hanging out while I was training. After being cut by my club, I was playing for a Group 6 first-grade league team, the Narellan Jets. I'd be running drills out on the field and I'd see my mates parked up on the hill, smoke curling out of the car windows. I'd find myself thinking, 'I can't wait to finish training and join them.' It became harder and harder to stop myself, and eventually, I just gave in to it. After I'd failed to make the cut for the Sharks and been dropped by Western Suburbs, I didn't bother resisting anymore.

What started as an occasional escape turned into a daily ritual. I'd wake up in the morning, skip breakfast and immediately start thinking about how to score my first session of the day. My mates and I would scrape together enough to buy a $20 bag. Once that session was done, the cycle started all over again. Our days revolved around the next session. If we weren't getting high, we were figuring out how to get high. We were young and dumb, and it was our way of escaping from all the problems of real life that we didn't know how to deal with.

One of my closest mates from that time, Mick, took his own life when he was just twenty-one or twenty-two. Mick's death was a gut punch for all of us. He had been a big part of the Airds community and losing him like that was a huge shock. But instead of talking about it or dealing with the loss, we all just doubled down on smoking every day, getting high to numb the grief. It was a stupid, destructive cycle.

Footy fell by the wayside, and my passion for the game dwindled. By the end of the season, I was benched during the grand final, a shadow of the player I'd been. I'd gone from a kid with a clear path to first grade to someone who wasn't even on the field. My fitness had suffered, my drive was gone and the game that had once defined me felt like it was out of reach. I tried to make a comeback a couple of years later, but the spark was gone. I wasn't the same player, and I knew it.

It's hard to come to terms with the promise I'd shown in comparison to where I ended up. I often think about the what-ifs: What if I'd stayed at Western Suburbs? What if I'd stayed away from marijuana? The regret stings, especially when I see players I trained alongside going on to play State of Origin and sign million-dollar contracts. It hurts knowing I could've been there, too, if I'd made different choices.

It's not an easy thing to admit, but I was lost. And when you're lost, it's easy to follow the wrong map. For me, Airds was full of distractions, and I grabbed on to the wrong ones. It's a dark chapter in my life, but it was also a crossroads. The decisions I made during that time shaped what came next, both good and bad.

•

In the middle of my stoner period, I found out I was going to be a dad. The news hit me like a truck.

Jane had gone overseas for a holiday over Christmas, and when she came back, she told me she was pregnant. I was nineteen, living life recklessly, and then, bam, everything changed. Or at least, it should have.

At the time, I was smoking marijuana daily and barely keeping myself together. I wasn't ready for fatherhood in any way at all – not mentally, not emotionally. Sadly, it didn't feel like a life-changing moment; it felt more like something I had to get through. I didn't process it properly, to be honest. Jane, on the other hand, seemed to take it all in stride. She knew exactly what she wanted and expected me to grow up, step up, get a job and start saving for a house. But I wasn't as disciplined or focused as I should have been.

We talked about marriage, but at that point, I think we were just trying to tackle the challenge of becoming parents. When her pregnancy progressed, we stayed at her mum and dad's house for a while. They were incredibly supportive, which made things a bit easier for both of us.

Looking back, I can see just how unprepared I was. Jane was pushing for stability and a future, while I was stuck in my own head, caught up in bad habits. I wish I'd been more present, more involved, but at that point, I was just trying to get by. Being a dad wasn't something I had planned for, but life doesn't always wait for you to be ready.

Jane was sick of my behaviour, and she wasn't shy about saying so. She told me point-blank that I was a no-hoper. 'You just smoke pot every day,' she said. 'We're not buying a house. There's no money.' For at least twelve months, she warned me to get my act together, to stop smoking and start taking life seriously. But I didn't listen. I'd come home stoned and try to hide it, using Clear Eyes to mask the signs. But she always knew. She'd take one look at me then turn and go to bed. I'd just sit there, stoned, feeling totally out of it.

The worst thing was, I didn't really care. My priorities were a mess. I'd hold a job for a few months, then let it slide while I hung out with my mates, getting high and avoiding responsibility. Meanwhile, Jane was working hard. She was reliable and driven, and always had a job. Back then, she worked at Supré. I'd drop her at work on a Sunday, then spend the rest of the day getting stoned. It was a vicious cycle, one I couldn't seem to break.

In 1995, Jayden was born. That should've been a wake-up call, the thing that made me turn my life around. But I was so deep in my habits that even becoming a dad didn't snap me out of my haze. We got our own place, tried to make a go of it, but I wasn't pulling my weight.

Eventually, Jane left me. She'd had enough. I moved back in with my parents, who were amazing to both me and Jane. Mum and Dad even gave her a car to get around. Even though we'd broken up, my parents still considered her family. That's just who they were: kind, nurturing people who always stepped up when someone needed help.

Jane's family were no different. As I mentioned before, I ended up living with them for a stint and got really close to them all – her parents and her brothers. They treated me like one of their own. I still chat to her mum now and then, and I was gutted when her dad passed away from cancer. He was a good man. A real gentleman.

One of her brothers, another top bloke, has stayed in touch over the years. Every once in a while, when things have been rough, he's sent a message just to check in. That's always meant a lot. They're good people, and I'll always be grateful for the time I had with them.

After the break-up, moving back into Mum and Dad's place didn't feel like much of a homecoming. It was more like treading water, just trying to keep my head above the emotional mess I was in. Living with my parents again wasn't exactly smooth sailing, either. They were old-school, always on me to get a job and sort myself out. But I was too deep in my rut to listen. I'd hide what I was doing as best I could, sneaking off to Airds to smoke with the boys and only coming home late at night. Looking back, I think they knew. Maybe they didn't have all the details, but they weren't stupid. Dad in particular wasn't shy about letting me know how he felt. He'd always tell me, 'Get a job, mate. You can't just sit around all day.' And Mum, sweet as she was, would prod me as well, hoping I'd pull myself together. Deep down, I knew they were right, that I was wasting years, even if I didn't want to admit it. At the time, I brushed it all off.

Despite everything, Jane and I stayed in touch. The romance was done, but she was still a part of my life because of Jayden. My parents, bless them, did their best to help us out. They were devoted to their grandson, and I think they stepped in where I fell short. I saw Jayden occasionally, but I wasn't the father I should've been. I was too caught up in my own downward spiral, and too blind to see what I was missing.

Looking back now, I wish I'd done things differently. I wish I'd been more present, more hands-on, and a better role model for Jayden. But the past is the past, and while I can't change it, I've worked hard to do better, and to be there for him in whatever way I can.

•

When I was twenty-three years old, I met a lovely woman. To be completely honest, I can't remember exactly where we met, which says a lot about the state of my life at the time. It was probably at a nightclub, but it's a bit of a blur. Within six months of us meeting, she fell pregnant.

Everything moved pretty quickly from there. After our daughter Shaylee was born, we decided to make a fresh start and moved up to Umina on the Central Coast.

It was beautiful up there: a slower pace, close to the beach. It felt like things were headed in the right direction, but I still had my struggles. It was laid out for me early on: either I quit smoking pot or we weren't going to work. At first, I tried to hide it, sneaking around and pretending I'd quit. But after about a year, I realised I couldn't keep that up – I was basically living a double life. I wanted to settle down, build a life and provide for my kids.

Giving up pot was tough, but that wasn't the only thing I struggled with during those years. I'd be at work, flipping through the sports section of the paper on my lunch break, and I'd see articles about my old footy mates signing million-dollar contracts, playing in the big leagues. It stung, seeing them in the paper and knowing I'd once been on the same path. It was hard to accept how far I'd strayed from those dreams.

That time helped me get my head straight. Being away from the old stomping grounds gave me a fresh start and the space to focus on family. We spent our days doing simple things – going to the beach, having friends over and just enjoying the slower pace. It felt simple, and normal – something I hadn't felt in years.

We'd also make the trip down the freeway a couple of times a month to pick up Jayden. He'd stay with us during the holidays, and we'd hang out at Umina Beach, playing in the sand or splashing in the waves. Around that time, I started training again – weights, fitness, anything to keep me active. Without marijuana clouding my days, my energy and drive came back.

Eventually, the training led me back to footy. At twenty-seven, I gave it another shot and tried out for the Canberra Raiders. I spent an off-season training with them down in Canberra, pushing myself to see if I still had it. Unfortunately, I got cut right at the end, but that experience was a lesson I'm grateful for. It reminded me that it was never too late to fight for something better.

As much as we loved Umina, after a while, it started to feel a bit isolating, and we decided to come back to Sydney. We found our own little place in St Helens Park. Not long after that, I landed a proper job with Toll, driving trucks and delivering parcels. It was steady work, and I enjoyed it. That job was a major turning point for me. I wasn't touching drugs anymore, and my focus was on providing for my family. Our goal was to save a deposit and buy a house. It was tough, though. Between rent, bills and looking after Jayden on weekends, money was always tight. Plus, our daughter Shaylee was now in the picture – a beautiful fun-loving little human who just changed my world. Such a joy for me.

I settled into being a dad pretty naturally this time around. It wasn't always easy, but it felt right. I was busy with the new job with Toll. I worked hard Monday to Friday, and when the weekend came, we made the most of it. Life had become all about family. We'd take Shaylee and Jayden to the movies or plan trips away. Some of my favourite memories from that time are the holidays we spent on the Gold Coast, hitting the theme parks or relaxing on the beach. We were always finding ways to enjoy life. It was a different pace from my younger days, and it felt good.

Once I got back into training with the Raiders, fitness also became a cornerstone of my life. Even after my time with the team ended, I stayed super fit and kept training regularly. It became a way of life, something that helped keep my head clear and my body strong.

I was twenty-nine by then, a different bloke from the years before. I'd got off the weed and built my fitness back up. On the surface, life looked settled. I had a steady job, I was training hard, spending weekends at the movies or on the Goldy with Shaylee and Jayden. But underneath all that, cracks were starting to show in my relationship.

We both tried hard to make it work, but the truth was that while we were both growing, we were growing in different directions. As hard as it was, we knew it wasn't going to work; it was time to call it. That was tough, but I feel lucky for the good times and for my gorgeous daughter, Shaylee.

5

THE GLOW BEFORE THE STORM

After the break-up, I leaned on my mate Russell, who offered me a weekend job with him at Tip Top delivering bread alongside my Monday-to-Friday gig at Toll. I wanted more financial security, and while working seven days a week was exhausting, it gave me purpose. I moved back in with Mum and Dad, who didn't charge me any rent, meaning I could save everything I earned. Every Wednesday, I'd stop at an ATM and check my bank balance. Seeing those numbers grow week by week kept me going. I managed to save $1300, then the balance got to $2600, and eventually

I had $18,000. I'd pin those slips to the dash of my truck as a reminder of why I was working so bloody hard.

By then, I was a different man from the one I had been in my early twenties. The bad habits and the aimlessness were gone. I never even thought about drugs anymore. I was 100 per cent focused on working hard and saving for a house. It felt like if I could achieve that, I could have some stability, and a better future.

My routine became pretty predictable: I'd finish my deliveries around 3 pm, grab some lunch, have a quick snooze in the truck and then hit the gym. It was my escape, an hour every day to just zone out and focus on myself.

My social life took a back seat during that time; most nights, I was too tired to do much more than head home and crash. But my hard work paid off – after eighteen months, I finally saved enough to buy a house in Ambarvale, not far from Mum and Dad's place.

Buying a house had been my dream for so long, and it felt pretty awesome to achieve that. Mum and Dad always credit me for that period of my life. Mum would often say, 'You wouldn't have got where you are without that effort, so well done.' It was a nice acknowledgement, but I couldn't have done it without their help.

At last, it seemed like my future had promise. I'm forever grateful to my parents for letting me live with them rent-free and feeding me the greatest home-cooked meals you could ever imagine. My mum used to pack me lunches every day, too. Life was great.

One thing I found really funny was how strict my dad was, even though I was twenty-nine by then. We still ate dinner together at the table every night, and you still weren't allowed to have your elbows on the table. And he had this rule where no-one could start eating until everyone was seated. It used to drive me mad because the food would go cold while we were waiting.

But, looking back, those lessons stuck with me. They taught me good manners and discipline, and I insist on a lot of the same rules with my own family today. It's something I appreciate now.

•

One day at the gym, I got chatting with a guy who always seemed to smell of something distinctive, like he was wearing some kind of lotion. One day, I asked him about it, and he laughed and told me it was something called Accelerate, a cream that helped you burn faster in the solarium. I'd never used a solarium before.

'Chicks dig it,' he added with a grin. I remember thinking, *Why not?*

I quickly became hooked. In the early 2000s, solariums seemed to be everywhere: in gyms, in salons, right next to the protein powders and tanning oils. I'd see a sign for one while I was out making a delivery, pull over and head in for a quick session. It became something I did without even really thinking about it, like stopping for fuel. I'd jump into a solarium for fifteen or twenty minutes, then get back in my truck and head to the next job.

There were two main types of solariums: lie-down beds and stand-up units. They were fitted with strong blue lights that looked a bit like oversized mosquito zappers, but they were much more intense. I'd always go in wearing my undies, never naked, and slot the coins into the machine.

The experience was intense. It was like being in a sauna, but instead of just sweating, you were roasting under the UV lights. The lie-down beds felt a bit claustrophobic, especially if you let your mind wander, but I didn't let it bother me. I kept my focus on the end result: looking good. That made it all worthwhile.

Most sessions lasted around seven or eight minutes, but I usually did double sessions, so I'd come out super toasted. Some people did triple sessions, but that seemed a bit over the top, even for me. Afterward, my skin would be red and raw, like a sunburn, but within a day or two, I'd have a fabulous deep tan. It lasted about four or five days before fading, so I'd top it up regularly, every five days without fail.

At the gym, I started getting compliments on my tan. I took pride in it. I was already training hard, getting fit and feeling good about myself, so the tan felt like the cherry on top. It wasn't just about looking good; it was about feeling good, too. And after the break-up, it gave me a much-needed confidence boost. I remember how much time I spent at the gym, always checking myself out in the mirrors. It's funny how the gym mirrors seem to exaggerate your progress, but even more so when you're tanned. You can see every muscle, every line, and that just made me want to keep going back for more.

Little did I know how much solariums would shape the next chapter of my life – and not in the way I expected. If I could go back and undo one decision, it would be stepping into that first solarium. No question about it. At the time, it seemed harmless. Just another thing to add to my routine. Something to boost the way I looked and felt about myself. I didn't stop to think about what it might be doing to me beyond that, and I had no reason to. I was chasing a tan, chasing confidence.

To this day, I regret it. I was using solariums without a second thought, and more importantly, without any real understanding of the risks. I'd give anything to go back and shake that version of myself, knock him around and tell him it's not worth it. No glow is worth gambling with your life.

•

Skin cancer was never something I thought about seriously. Back then, it just didn't seem like a real threat. That changed when I heard about Clare Oliver in 2007.

I first saw her on TV, on *60 Minutes*. The footage showed Clare in her hospital room, looking out the window at the sunlight glinting off the glass. It must've felt like a cruel joke – that beautiful sunlight was the thing that was killing her.

She was only twenty-six, but she was facing the end of her life because of something most of us barely gave a second thought to: melanoma. It's a cancer that doesn't muck around, but it does sneak up on you. It sits there in your skin, burrowing into your cells, while you just go about your life, clueless. For Clare, it had already done its worst. She knew the score.

I remember seeing Clare's face and feeling like the wind had been knocked out of me. This young woman was sitting there talking about death like it was just around the corner – because it was. It shook me. She wasn't some old person with wrinkled skin who'd lived a long life and run out of luck. Clare was around the same age as me, and it felt like she was looking straight through the camera and talking directly to me. I couldn't have known it then, but in less than six months, I would be in a hospital bed just like hers, fighting my own battle with melanoma.

I'd grown up in a time when sunburn was just part of summer. You'd roast at the beach, peel for a week and then do it all again the next weekend. The darker the tan, the better. Then we added solariums into the mix. No-one thought it was dangerous. It was just part of the scene.

But Clare changed that. Her words hit hard. This wasn't some doctor preaching about UV rays; it was someone just like me who was living with it. Dying of it. Clare had believed the same things I believed. That tanning was harmless. That cancer was something other people got.

In a matter of weeks, Clare Oliver became a household name. It wasn't that she was chasing the spotlight; it was that she had something to say. She didn't want anyone else to end up in a hospital bed because they'd wanted a tan.

Clare had fair skin, dark hair. She was full of spark, loved her life. And like so many other people, she loved that sun-kissed look – the glow, the bronzed skin, the 'healthy' vibe it gave off. Back in the early 2000s, that glow was everything. Magazines, TV ads and beauty pages all pushed the same idea: that having a tan meant you were fit and beautiful, that you had your life together. And Clare had bought into it, just as I had.

It wasn't until 2004, when she was just twenty-two, that Clare noticed a mole on her back. It was small at first, easy to ignore. But then it changed. It got bigger and darker – uglier. By the time she got it checked, it had already spread to her liver, lungs and bones. It was stage 4. Terminal.

But Clare wasn't the type to just sit back and let it happen. She wasn't going to go quietly. By 2007, after going through several rounds of chemo while her body copped hit after hit, she made a decision. She was going to speak up. Not just for herself, but for everyone else being sold the lie that tanning was harmless.

She wrote a letter to Australia and laid it all out. No fluff, no sugar-coating. Just the truth.

'I want to make my message clear,' she wrote. 'Don't use solariums. Don't tan yourself on purpose. It is not worth your life.'

And people listened. Mate, did they listen.

Her words hit hard. You couldn't turn on the TV or flick through the paper without seeing Clare's face, tired but determined. Sometimes her voice cracked, but you could always hear the fire in it. She didn't want pity. She wanted change.

Clare passed away on 13 September 2007. She didn't live long enough to see how her words rippled out to make change, but she knew her message had landed. She knew people were paying attention. And that's the thing – she turned the worst chapter of her life into something powerful. Something that still matters.

While Clare may have lost her life to melanoma, her voice didn't fade. In the months after her death, change started to happen. By December 2007, just three months later, the Victorian Government announced major reforms to the solarium industry. These changes weren't symbolic gestures – they were real and enforceable. New laws made it compulsory for solarium operators to be licensed and mandated that health warnings about the dangers of skin cancer be displayed prominently in every facility. For the first time, the industry was being held accountable.

The changes didn't stop there. In February 2009, the Victorian Government went further: state legislation was introduced banning anyone under the age of eighteen from using solariums. It was a landmark moment, thanks to Clare's brave campaigning in her final weeks. She had given melanoma a face, a voice and a story.

But despite the new legislation, not all solarium operators were doing the right thing. Enforcement was still patchy, and plenty of them cut corners, putting profit first. And outside Victoria, change was yet to happen in the same way. That's where people like me, inspired by Clare, picked up her mission. The awareness she raised laid the groundwork for our campaigns. Today still, in all the work I do, I'm amplifying Clare's message and making sure her warning never fades.

Clare didn't just fight for her life. She fought for ours, and even after she was gone, she kept winning battles. Every new law, every shut-down solarium and every life saved from melanoma is part of her legacy.

Ask anyone who knew her and they'll tell you she was tough, smart, funny and full of heart. She didn't go down without a fight. And she wasn't just fighting for herself. Clare fought for every teenager stepping into a tanning bed, every young bloke thinking sunburn's no big deal, every parent who never thought skin cancer would touch their kid.

To this day, Clare's story echoes. It reminds us that melanoma doesn't discriminate. That beauty isn't worth dying for. That your life is worth more than a tan.

Watching her speak out in her final days, seeing how hard she was fighting just to be heard, made me pause.

For the first time, I looked at my own skin and wondered, *What the hell have I been doing?*

Clare's story stuck with me. It sat there in the back of my mind, and when I was diagnosed with melanoma myself only a few months later, her voice came roaring back. I thought about the way she used her last breath to try and save others, and how I'd spent so long pretending I was bulletproof, only to realise I wasn't. That none of us are.

Clare made melanoma impossible to ignore. And in some weird way, even though I never met her, she made sure I took my own diagnosis seriously. Eventually, she also helped me speak up and share my story, to stop others from going through what I did.

She was a hero, simple as that. Not because she was perfect or polished, but because she was brave enough to speak the truth when it mattered most. That truth changed me forever, and I'm proud to be a part of the wave that she started.

6
SILVER COMMODORE, GOLDEN GIRL

I met Janine in 2006, when I was thirty-one.

Our first meeting was a bit of a disaster. We saw each other in a car park and I tried to start a conversation, even asked for her number, but she knocked me back. I remember her saying, 'It's a bit random, don't you think?' I was mortified and got out of there quickly, my ego bruised. But three months later, fate brought us back together. I was at the club with a mate, playing the pokies, when I spotted her again. This time, we ended up talking. Her friends invited me over, and as we got chatting that night, Janine asked, 'Do you drive a silver Commodore?

Were you trying to pick me up in the car park?' I laughed, tried to deny it at first, but eventually I owned up. By the end of the night, I had her number. That turned out to be the start of something special.

Janine brought a new energy into my life, and I started making changes so I could spend more time with her. I cut back on weekend shifts, keeping Saturdays for us. It felt like a reward after all those months of hard work and sacrifice, a chance to slow down and start building something new.

The house I'd bought in Ambarvale, not far from Mum and Dad's, was a three-bedroom place with an in-ground pool – a real bachelor pad. I was so proud of it. I threw myself into fixing it up, really making it mine. I had the house rendered in grey, repainted the roof tiles and added timber doors and a new letterbox. Inside, I set up a TV with a surround sound system and got the place looking modern and stylish. I loved working on the house. After a long day at work, I couldn't wait to get home and pick up where I'd left off, whether it was painting, gardening or planning the next project.

That house became my sanctuary, and it made me feel like I'd achieved something. It wasn't just a home; it was a reflection of all my hard work, both in my career and my personal life. And meeting Janine felt like the beginning of a new chapter, one I hadn't been expecting.

Janine and I hit it off pretty quickly. She was stunning – blonde hair, blue eyes, just beautiful – and I felt really lucky. I'd already booked a trip to the US for Christmas before meeting her, so I asked her if she wanted to come, even though we'd only been together for about three months. She said yes, and I decided to shout her the trip. I had money saved up, and I wanted to share the experience with her. We spent about fifteen days backpacking through Hollywood and Las Vegas, and it was amazing.

My kids also loved Janine. They got along really well, and she embraced them as if they were her own. There was no hesitation on her part; she just took them in and treated them like family. That meant everything to me.

Janine ended up moving in before we even went away – by then, she was over at my place every day, anyway. I said, 'Why don't you move in?' and that was that. Simple. She started working nearby, doing nails as a beautician. Life was good.

I'd love to say that the moment I saw Clare Oliver's story, I walked out of the solarium and never went back, but that would be a lie. I kept going. Not straight away, and not without thinking about Clare, but still, I continued going regularly. A tan made me feel good about myself, and I wanted to keep Janine interested, so I was trying to stay in shape and maintain that healthy glow.

Clare made melanoma real – there was no doubt about that. But even reality doesn't break a routine straight away. And when I saw Clare on TV, I was already addicted. I could walk into that blue-lit room for eight minutes, come out red raw, and in just a few days, I'd feel better about what I saw in the mirror. It sounds ridiculous, I know, especially after seeing what Clare went through, but I wasn't ready to let go of that version of myself. I didn't know how to.

Clare's story stayed with me. I thought about her more than I was willing to admit back then. But the thing is, tanning wasn't just a habit; it had become part of who I was, totally wrapped up in how I saw myself. Solariums were in every gym, still legal, still booked out. So I kept going. I told myself I'd stop soon, I'd just top it up one more time. Just one more session before the weekend, before the next gym sesh. Just one more. It's hard to think about now, but I kept going to solariums right up until my melanoma diagnosis. The last time I used one was just a week before I went to see Doctor Gupta about the mole on my left ankle. I was in the solarium, taking my socks off beforehand, and noticed the mole was bleeding and itchy. I thought, *Shit, that doesn't look too good*. But even then, I still went ahead with the session. I was hooked. Looking good meant feeling good, and that bronze glow felt like armour.

This stuff runs deep in Aussie culture. We grew up thinking tanned skin was proof that you were doing life right. If you weren't bronzed, you were sick, lazy or hadn't been outdoors enough. A tan brought confidence. And for someone like me, who'd already had my self-esteem knocked around a bit, that tan was like a shield. When you've spent years rebuilding your life, chasing stability and trying to outrun your own shadow, sometimes you cling to the things that make you feel whole, even when you know they could be destroying you.

•

I had also found comfort and confidence in my relationship with Janine, especially once she moved in. Being with Janine was like finally being seen for who I really was. She wasn't just my girlfriend; she was my person.

We got engaged late in 2007.

Proposing to Janine was one of the best decisions I ever made. It was before everything – before the cancer, before the hospitals, before the cameras started rolling. At that point, life still felt full of momentum and possibility. We were happy, in love, just living in our little bubble. I didn't go down on one knee with a big speech or anything, but it was real. It meant something. I'd found someone who saw the best in me, even when I didn't always see it in myself, and I didn't want to let her go.

We planned our engagement party for early in the new year, full of hope for the future.

I'd had this mole on my ankle for a while by then – it just wouldn't heal. It'd bleed, scab over and then start all over again. Janine started urging me to get it checked. Honestly, if it wasn't for her, I might never have gone to the doctor. She'd been on my case for months, pointing it out constantly.

And every time, I'd try to laugh it off, thinking that being tanned and fit was all that mattered. But she could see past all that. She saw how red and burnt I'd get after using solariums. She'd shake her head and say, 'What are you doing to yourself? Look at how burnt you are. This isn't good for you.'

It all came to a head when we were planning another trip to the US. Janine put her foot down. 'We're not going anywhere unless you get that checked first.' Looking back, it's clear that Janine's insistence probably saved my life. I hadn't been ready to face what it might mean, but she didn't give me a choice, thank god.

As Christmas approached, I finally listened. Reluctantly, I booked an appointment with my GP and showed him my ankle. He took one look at it and said, 'This needs to come out straight away.' There was no hesitation in his voice, and that made me pause. He said it didn't look good, and he wanted to act quickly.

I had the mole removed, but even then, I wasn't worried. I figured it was just a precaution. The procedure felt routine. The medical staff numbed the area around the mole and removed it. I wasn't overly concerned. I thought, *It's just something small, life goes on.*

A few days later, Janine and I were hosting a barbecue with friends when I got *the* call. It was around 5.30 in the afternoon. My doctor's voice was serious. 'Jay, you need to come in,' he said. 'The results have come back. It's melanoma.'

7

CAMERAS, COMMITMENT AND CANCER

When I think about it now, it's wild how calm I was. I didn't panic or fall apart. I was just . . . numb. I think I heard the word 'melanoma' but didn't fully grasp what it meant. I'd heard the word before, sure, but even after hearing Clare Oliver's story just a few months earlier, it didn't set off alarm bells.

Looking back, I can see that when Doctor Gupta gave me the news, it didn't sink in immediately. He didn't sugar-coat it, he gave it to me straight: *melanoma, needs urgent attention, see a specialist.* His tone was serious, more serious than I'd ever heard from him. But still I brushed it off, thinking, *Righto, they'll cut it out and that'll be that.* Like it was no big deal.

When we drove over to the clinic that night, Janine and I were both calm. There were still guests at our house from the barbecue we'd been hosting, and I remember thinking, *We'll go get this sorted and head straight back.* But when we walked in and saw the look on Doctor Gupta's face, things started to feel different. He was rattled. And *that* rattled me.

He said, 'Jay, this is serious. You should have come to me earlier.' He didn't need to join the dots; I understood what he was saying. Even then, though, it felt like it was happening to someone else. Janine held my hand. She was always the glass-half-full one, and I leaned on that – pretty heavily at times.

It was only much later, after having the scans and seeing the specialists and hearing things like 'T2 melanoma' and 'lymphatic spread' that it hit me. But even driving home from the doctor's that night, I still believed everything would be fine. I was downplaying it to myself, thinking, *It's on my ankle, it's not like it's in my heart.* I was trying to rationalise it, like I was still invincible, like it couldn't really be happening to me. That's the thing about denial: it's comfortable.

Deep down, my body had been trying to tell me the truth – I just hadn't been listening. That weird feeling under my skin late at night, the restlessness, the way I couldn't shake the feeling that something was wrong . . . I'd ignored all the signs. I'd written it off as a blister. Just my boot rubbing my ankle. No big deal. But it turned out to be a pretty big deal.

Cancer doesn't always announce itself. Sometimes it just lurks quietly until someone says it out loud, and then suddenly it's everywhere. Once the word was spoken, it hung over everything. The past. The future. All the choices I'd made, all the things I'd been planning. The whole lot.

At that moment, it was like I split into two people. There was the me who was carefree and breezy and thought nothing serious could ever happen, and then there was the me sitting in that doctor's office, nodding slowly, pretending to be okay.

But I wasn't okay. Not even close.

•

Two weeks later, I went to see a cancer specialist, Doctor Quinn, at the Sydney Melanoma Unit in North Sydney.

Doctor Quinn introduced himself and pulled up a chair across from me. He was calm and straight to the point – the kind of bloke who made you sit up and listen. He pulled up my pathology report and talked me through the details. The tumour was 1.95 millimetres thick, he told me. I didn't know what that meant at the time, but he explained that anything over one millimetre is serious – it means the melanoma has probably reached the second layer of the skin.

Doctor Quinn patiently outlined how melanoma works: when it reaches a certain depth, cells can break away and get into your lymphatic system or bloodstream, forming new tumours in other parts of your body – something called 'metastasis'. He said, 'There's a chance it could have spread. If it has, there aren't many treatments available. Once melanoma spreads, it's often a death sentence.'

He explained that the next step was for me to have a lymphoscintigraphy scan. They'd inject a radioactive dye into the skin near the scar, then track where the dye travelled through my lymphatic system. Wherever the dye landed first, that was the sentinel node – the one most likely to catch melanoma cells if they'd started spreading. If it lit up, they'd remove it during surgery and send it off for testing. It was the best way to know if the cancer had started spreading beyond the skin.

Then he added the part that really shook me: 'It could be in your liver, lungs or brain.' I felt all the blood drain from my face. The idea that cancer could travel through your blood or lymphatic system to critical organs, your liver, your lungs, your brain, was terrifying.

It's hard to describe that moment. There's a certain gravity that hits when you have to face your own mortality. I remember thinking, *This is real. This isn't something you just shake off.*

It didn't help that Doctor Quinn's bedside manner was not warm. It felt like he was telling me off. His words were matter-of-fact, but his tone seemed to say, *Dude, wake up. You've done this to yourself.* It was harsh. Looking back, maybe that's what I needed, but at the time, his words cut deep.

The appointment left me pretty rattled. I remember driving home with Janine, trying to get my mind around what he'd told me. She tried to reassure me, like she always did, saying, 'You'll be fine. We'll just take it one step at a time,' but it was clear she was worried, too.

I lost two kilos in the following week, just from the stress. I couldn't eat properly. I couldn't sleep. My mind was racing. I couldn't stop thinking, *Am I going to die?*

At the end of that first visit to his office, Doctor Quinn had explained that he couldn't feel any swollen lymph nodes during his examination, but I'd still need to undergo the lymphoscintigraphy scan, a lymphocytogram. He scheduled the procedure for 14 February. Valentine's Day. I'd have to wait another excruciating two months until then.

•

A few days later, Doctor Quinn called with more news, a very different kind this time. 'We've had an inquiry from Channel 9's *RPA* TV show – they're interested in documenting your story.'

RPA was one of those shows I used to flick past on TV and sometimes get drawn into. It followed the day-to-day goings-on at RPA in Sydney, with cameras rolling as people came in with everything from broken bones to life-threatening illnesses. There was no fancy editing, just raw, honest footage of what goes on behind the scenes in one of the country's busiest hospitals. Real patients and real doctors. You saw people at their most vulnerable, and the doctors and nurses doing everything they could to help them. It was confronting at times, but always powerful. Doctor Quinn told me that stories like mine, things that viewers could relate to, were the kind they liked to feature on the show.

At first, I didn't quite know what to make of the idea. I mean, who even thinks about going through their entire medical journey on camera? But Doctor Quinn thought it might help raise awareness of melanoma, and honestly, part of me also thought, *Well, this might be kind of cool.*

Janine and I sat with it overnight, just to make sure we were both comfortable with the whole idea and with sharing our lives on TV. On the surface, yeah, the thought of being on telly was a bit of a novelty, and something we joked about. But more than that, I agreed with Doctor Quinn that if my story could help educate others and maybe get even one person to book in a skin check or think twice about tanning, then it was worth doing.

We didn't really overthink it. There was so much going on as it was, and I just wanted to get the ball rolling so we could get on with life. I figured, if I was going through it anyway, why not let the cameras film it? It would be a welcome distraction from my growing fear about what was happening inside my body. Besides, I kind of liked the idea of being on television.

Not long after I agreed to do the show, the lead producer, Carol, got in touch. She was lovely and put me at ease straight away. She asked about Janine and me. 'I hear you're getting married soon?' she said. 'We'd love to cover that as well, if it fits.' We were in the middle of planning our wedding, and our engagement party was just around the corner. It would make great television, Carol told me.

The whole thing felt very surreal. Here I was, trying to wrap my mind around a cancer diagnosis, and then suddenly I had signed up to share my private life with a TV audience. But I thought that maybe documenting everything might help me process it all.

•

Despite the diagnosis and the procedure I had coming up, we went ahead with the engagement party in January. We had it at our house in Ambarvale. It was fabulous being surrounded by all our friends and family, but also kind of bittersweet. True, we were celebrating love and commitment, but there was a shadow hanging over us.

I didn't appreciate it at the time, but that was one of the last moments before it all really began. I was staring down the barrel of a truckload of scans, biopsies and imaging so they could work out if and how far the cancer had spread. My life was about to become completely over-whelming. I'd honestly expected that they'd cut out the mole, stitch me up, and life would carry on. I couldn't have been more wrong.

Even looking back now, everything in those first few months after receiving the diagnosis is a bit of a blur. I truly believed I might not have had much time left. It was as if a clock had started ticking, and there was this constant, low-level panic running underneath everything we did. We had to make decisions about the wedding during that time, too – how big it would be, where it would be held, who to invite – all while this dark cloud of uncertainty hovered above us. Would I even be able to attend? *RPA* filmed the entire journey from the melanoma diagnosis, and they planned to follow us until the wedding day. It became a series, a snapshot of our life during one of the most challenging times we'd ever faced.

And just as we were navigating the doctors, the scans, the dates and planning a wedding, Janine discovered she was pregnant. She was around six weeks along when we found out, and it felt like everything stopped for a second. We were stunned, overwhelmed with emotion, but for a happy reason this time. It was a moment of joy tangled up in the fear. On the one hand, it was the most incredible news, a sign that life was still moving forward in spite of everything. On the other hand, I couldn't help but think, *What if I'm not here to meet our baby?* Shit. From that point on, Janine's pregnancy and my treatment ran side by side. Every hospital appointment, every sleepless night, every little moment of hope or fear, we were experiencing it together, through two lenses: one of a tiny new life on the way and one of survival.

8

INTO THE SYSTEM

The lead-up to 14 February was a blur. I kept working, trying to convince myself that everything would be fine, that there was nothing to worry about. I even showed my boss the mark on my ankle from where the mole had first been removed, casually saying, 'I've got to get this melanoma checked out, but I'll be back next week.' I truly believed it would be a quick procedure, no big deal. Then I'd be back at work and life would return to normal.

But I never went back.

From then on, my reality changed completely. My days were filled with procedures, tests, recovery and a whole bundle of emotions. Looking back now, I had absolutely no idea what I was in for that day I first met with Doctor Quinn.

On the big day itself, Janine and I arrived at the hospital early, a bundle of nerves. Walking into RPA for the first time felt like stepping into another world. The place was totally spotless – white walls and shiny floors. It was so clinical, there was absolutely no warmth in it. I was surrounded by the noise of machines, beeping monitors, announcements coming through the speakers. There were nurses rushing around everywhere. I felt completely out of place.

Just days earlier, I'd been at work, mucking around with the boys, thinking about footy and what to cook for dinner. One day, you're planning a future. The next, you're wondering if you even have one.

The camera crew was already there, waiting. They mic'd us up straight away – me, Janine and even some of the hospital staff. It felt surreal. Walking through the hospital corridors with a sound guy, a cameraman and the producer made the whole thing feel more like a film set than a hospital. There were lights and wires everywhere, and the crew were getting directions through their earpieces. It was overwhelming, but I think, in some strange way, the distraction helped.

At first, I was more nervous about being filmed than I was about the procedure. Every single thing I said and did was being recorded. I'd never been on TV before, and I couldn't help feeling self-conscious. But after a while, the cameras started to fade into the background and the reason I was there took over. This wasn't just a story for a TV show; it was *my* story. This was my life.

I hadn't watched a lot of *RPA* before this, but I was familiar with the show – it was always on in the background at home. Janine and I were genuinely excited to share our story. We told everyone about it: family, friends, workmates. The fact that my battle with melanoma would be shown on national television made the whole thing feel bigger than me. Like I wasn't just going through it for myself anymore – I was going through it for everyone who was watching, too.

I was desperately hoping that sharing my story would mean something. Maybe someone watching at home might decide to get a skin check, or cancel their next solarium session. The thought helped, if only slightly.

There was no payment involved, but we did receive a $500 David Jones voucher, which was generous. But honestly, the experience itself was worth far more. It gave me purpose, a chance to warn others about melanoma.

I was keen to use my struggle to help someone else if I could.

Before the scan, I met with Doctor Quinn again. That was a tough appointment, because he told me the depth of my melanoma meant I was in the T2 group. I learned that the 'T' stands for 'tumour thickness'. 'T2' means the melanoma is sitting somewhere between one and two millimetres deep. It doesn't sound like much – the size of a sewing-pin head, if that – but in the world of melanoma, it's deep. It meant the cancer had pushed past the surface of my skin and was starting to dig deeper. Once it's past that point, it can spread through your body, and that's when it gets dangerous. It wasn't the worst stage, but it wasn't the best, either. Out of 100 people with a T2 melanoma, around eighty-nine would still be alive in five years . . . and eleven wouldn't. That stuck with me. I couldn't stop picturing a room with 100 people and wondering which one I was.

My head was spinning. I didn't understand all the science, but I could tell it was serious.

Then, as I was waiting for the lymphocytogram to begin, I noticed some paperwork on a nearby desk. Clearly, I wasn't meant to see it. In bold print, I saw the words: *Stage 3 Melanoma.*

My stomach dropped. My mouth went dry, and I turned to Janine, my voice shaky. 'Stage 3? There's only four stages.

Holy hell, this is serious.' I was hoping Janine would tell me I'd got it wrong, that I'd misunderstood, but the look on her face said everything. I felt like I was freefalling.

The *RPA* crew was still filming, but suddenly I couldn't hear them anymore. Everything around me – the crew, the noise of the hospital, the chatter of the nurses – all blurred into the background. All I could hear was the roar of panic in my ears. I'd known I had melanoma, but finding out it was stage 3 gave it a whole new weight.

It wasn't until later that I realised I'd got it wrong.

What I'd actually seen that day on the paperwork wasn't 'stage 3' at all. It said *Clark level 3*, a term I hadn't heard at the time. To my untrained eye, and in the headspace I was in, I saw the number three next to the word 'melanoma' and jumped to the worst conclusion.

Clark levels are what doctors use to describe how deep a melanoma has grown into the layers of the skin. They go from level 1 (just on the surface) to level 5 (deep into the lower layers). Level 3, which is what I was at that point, meant the melanoma had grown into the skin's dermis, but hadn't yet gone deeper. It was serious, but it wasn't the same as stage 3, which means the cancer has spread to the lymph nodes and beyond.

The mix-up may have been small, but it was wild how it sent me into a full-blown spiral, all caught on camera.

The filming added a strange layer to an already over-whelming day. As I sat there trying to take in what the doctors were telling me, I could hear the crew moving around behind me, cables being dragged across the floor and the camera clicking. The doctors walked me through each step of the scan, explaining what they were going to do. I nodded along, but I wasn't really taking it in. It sounds like a cliché, but it felt like I was watching myself from above, like I was acting in someone else's medical documentary.

Finally, the procedure got started. They laid me down on the table and injected a radioactive dye into my ankle, where the melanoma had been. Looking at the screen, I could see the dye entering my body – it was black. I held my breath, waiting to see if the cancer cells had spread. It moved up from my ankle and into my groin. Part of me wanted to look away, but I couldn't stop staring.

Then, three lymph nodes lit up like tiny black marbles, impossible to ignore.

Doctor Quinn wasn't mucking around. He said, 'I recommend you come back this afternoon to get those lymph nodes removed.' It was clear it wasn't really a recommendation. It was an order, and I agreed immediately. 'Do what you've got to do,' I told him.

And that was it. Just like that, I was headed for surgery, a sentinel lymph node biopsy – no time to process or think it through. That Valentine's Day was quickly turning into the most important day of my life – and probably the least romantic.

•

I learned later on that not every patient has their lymph nodes removed straight away. Sometimes the nodes are monitored for a while to see if they grow or change before deciding whether to take action. But for me, that just wasn't an option. Doctor Quinn didn't hesitate. Turns out, his swift action was what saved my life.

I wouldn't know it for another week, but when they analysed the lymph nodes after surgery, they found microscopic traces of melanoma in one of them. The cancer had spread from my ankle to my groin. It was official: this thing was on the move. And it didn't stop there. They had also taken a wider section of skin from around the original melanoma site on my ankle. When they examined it, they found another cluster of melanoma cells, just beginning to break through into the surrounding tissue.

If Doctor Quinn had waited even a few weeks, those cells could have kept spreading. If we had decided to wait and see what happened, there's every chance it would have got into my liver, my lungs or my brain within months. I'd dodged a bullet – no, more like a cannonball.

Through all this, somehow, Janine stayed calm. She held my hand, kept her voice soft and steady, reminding me to breathe, to stay grounded, to take things one step at a time. It was easier said than done, of course, but her presence kept me from completely unravelling.

Coming out of surgery, Janine's voice was the first thing I heard, distant at first – I was still foggy from the anaesthetic – but unmistakably hers. Soft. Reassuring. And when I finally opened my eyes, there she was, leaning over me. It was like coming out of a storm and heading into calm waters.

The operation itself had been painless – after all, I'd been out cold under general anaesthetic. But the recovery was something else. I was sore, foggy and scared. My leg was bandaged and strapped, with a surgical drain coming out of the wound. I'd walked into the hospital under my own steam and woken up attached to tubes, with no idea what the future held.

It was still Valentine's Day, and even in the thick of my fear and discomfort, I wanted to do something special for Janine. We were engaged, after all. The future suddenly seemed very uncertain, but I was keen to hold tightly to the pieces of it we still had. Even though I was surrounded by beeping monitors and fluorescent lights, I thought, *Let's still mark this day. Let's remind ourselves what we're fighting for.*

So I organised a Valentine's tray of food to be brought up to us. It wasn't much, just the standard hospital fare dressed up with a little heart-shaped garnish, but it meant something. It was my way of showing Janine that even though everything felt upside down, I hadn't forgotten about us. Love doesn't pause for illness. If anything, it deepens.

That night, sore and dazed from surgery, I sat beside Janine, sharing hospital lasagne and jelly cups as if they were a five-star meal. It wasn't about the food; it was about making a moment. Something that was just for us in the middle of this scary day in hospital. A glimmer of normal life in a situation that felt anything but. It gave us both something to hold on to.

When Janine left that night, something in me cracked. Up until that point, I'd tried to keep up a brave front. For Janine. For my family. Even for the cameras. But alone in that hospital bed, with a drain poking out of my leg, surrounded by unfamiliar noises, the fear caught up with me. The drain was a constant, physical reminder that something was happening to me that I couldn't control.

It was foreign and weird. Every movement knocked it or tugged on it, and every tug was like a reminder: *This is serious.*

The doctor's words kept playing in my head. *It could have spread.* I couldn't stop thinking about those words. I tried to distract myself, and I tried using logic to calm myself down, but nothing helped. I lay there thinking, *I'm only thirty-two. This can't be it. I've barely started. I don't want to die.* It was the first time I'd felt completely powerless.

The night dragged on; I couldn't sleep. The hours seemed to stretch out forever, and I'd never felt more alone in my life.

But even in the thick of all the fear I was feeling, there was one thought I kept coming back to: *I wasn't done yet.* I had Janine. I had my family. They needed me. I had so much more to do. I didn't know how I was going to get through it yet, but I knew I had to.

The next morning, I felt okay, although I was a bit tender, bruised and carrying a few extra stitches. But emotionally, I was carrying a new weight. The sentinel lymph node biopsy had been the first major operation. Now it was a waiting game.

•

When *RPA* had first reached out, they told me, 'Just pretend the cameras aren't there. We're just going to watch, just you, the doctors and Janine.' It sounded easy enough. And I did get used to them surprisingly quickly. By the time my next appointment rolled around a week later, when I was due to get the results of the biopsy, the crew were just part of the background.

However, they'd become a great indicator of what to expect, and when we arrived at the hospital a week after the surgery, I could tell something was off. The crew, usually chatty and relaxed, were subdued and quiet. They mic'd us up as they had the times before, but there was none of the usual banter. I couldn't shake the feeling that they knew something I didn't. Every second stretched out for an eternity – it was agonising. Minutes felt like hours. I whispered to Janine, 'What's going on? Can't they just tell us already?'

The sound guy was adjusting his equipment, and the doctor and producer were still out of the room, taking what felt like forever. I turned to the sound guy, my impatience getting the better of me. 'What's the hold-up? I just want to get my results. What's going on?' He tried to reassure me, saying, 'Oh, they're coming, they're coming,' but I could hear the unease in his voice. Something was up.

Later, I found out they already had the results. When they left the room, claiming they were waiting on the fax machine, they'd actually been discussing how to break the news to me. They were probably trying to work out how to make sure I was okay while still capturing the moment successfully for TV.

Finally, Doctor Quinn walked in and his face gave it away immediately – there was no need for words. I could see it written all over him: it was bad news. As he sat down, the silence was deafening. When he finally spoke, it was like the floor fell out from under me.

As was his style, he didn't sugar-coat it. 'Look, it's not good news,' he said. 'The melanoma has affected your lymphatic system. It's spread to one lymph node in your groin.' The extent of the spread classified it as stage 3 melanoma, he told me.

My stomach dropped. I gripped the arms of the chair so hard my knuckles turned white. After misreading that paperwork before my first scan, here I was being told I had stage 3 melanoma after all. It didn't feel real.

Given what they currently knew about the spread, Doctor Quinn said, I could have a sixty per cent chance of surviving the next five years. If the melanoma had advanced throughout my body, the odds were much worse. Hearing those numbers out loud, I couldn't even begin to understand the weight of what I was being told. Five years? I saw flashes of everything I would miss. Seeing my kids grow up. Growing old with Janine. Missing out on our beautiful life together.

Then he landed the final blow, clear and direct: 'There aren't many treatment options if melanoma spreads. You could die.'

The room blurred. I felt the blood drain from my face and everything went muffled, like I was underwater.

Janine was beside me, holding my hand, rubbing my back, but I barely even registered it. The cameras were still rolling, the boom mic hovering above us. I remember thinking, *How the hell is this my life?*

Doctor Quinn told me I'd need to come back for a bigger, riskier operation. They'd need to remove more lymph nodes from my groin. This surgery would be more invasive, with a much longer recovery time.

I nodded numbly, not really sure what I was agreeing to. All I could think was: *This thing wants to kill me.*

Something inside me broke then. I realised I was starting to cry – not sobbing, just silent tears welling up in my eyes. I was petrified.

Eventually, the appointment wrapped up. The film crew packed up their gear, carefully winding up cables and unhooking mics, just doing their jobs, but it all seemed like a sideshow now, like a strange parallel universe. Inside me, all I felt was chaos.

Doctor Quinn cleared me to go home and rest before the next surgery, saying they'd need me back in two weeks. It felt like I was going home to wait for the guillotine to fall.

'Take it easy,' he said. 'You need to give your body a chance to heal.' But rest seemed impossible. My mind wouldn't stop racing, and the idea of going back to our quiet house, just me and Janine, alone with our thoughts, was out of the question. I needed to be around people.

Driving home that day, the fear didn't subside. I stared out the window, watching the world go by and thinking, *Why can't I be that person walking down the street? Why can't I have their normal life? Why is this happening to me?* My mind kept circling back to one thought: *I'm going to die.*

Janine suggested we stay at her mum's house in Narellan Vale, and I jumped at the idea. It just made sense. Her mum was caring and warm, and the house just felt like home. There were family photos on the walls, the smell of home-cooked meals lingering in the air. It was a comforting place to be. We packed a bag and headed straight there. As soon as I stepped through the front door, there was a tiny wave of relief. I still didn't know what was coming, but at least I wouldn't be facing it alone.

Still, those two weeks were hell. I couldn't sit still. I was constantly on edge, flipping between numbness and full-blown panic. For the first time in my life, I started using a computer – I borrowed Janine's mum's computer so I could google what the hell I was dealing with. Before that, I didn't even have an email address. I was never a fan of technology. But now, I was clicking through page after page, searching for reassurance and hope. Instead, I found horror.

Every search seemed to bring up the same grim prognosis. Clare Oliver's story was everywhere. I couldn't escape it. She was young and vibrant – and then she was gone in a flash. I must've read her obituary a dozen times. I'd click away from the open tab, stare at the ceiling, then go straight back to it. I couldn't help myself.

I stumbled onto some online chat groups, connecting with people from all over the world. Those conversations helped. Just knowing there were others out there who understood what I was going through made a difference.

But I couldn't sleep. Every time I closed my eyes, I saw the word 'terminal'. I imagined my own funeral, and pictured Janine alone. I thought of my parents, of Jayden and Shaylee, and the new baby on the way. I couldn't stop thinking about the cancer growing inside me.

Janine was rock-solid, holding it together when I couldn't. She kept trying to reassure me, talking me through everything I was feeling, reminding me I was strong, that we weren't giving up. But even her words, as steady as they were, couldn't silence the voice in my head. *You're running out of time.*

And for the first time, I really believed it.

9

THE TEARS COME AT NIGHT

While waiting for my next surgery, I could barely think about anything else. I called one of the *RPA* producers at one point, begging for more information. 'Mate,' I said, 'you know when the doctor said it spread from my ankle to my groin? Do you think it's gone further? Can you go back and check the footage?'

He must've thought I'd lost it. 'Call your doctor, Jay,' he replied gently. But in that haze of fear, the crew were who I turned to. They'd become my allies, I guess. Strange as it might sound, I trusted them. They weren't just there for the story; they were kind, caring people. They weren't just media – they were human, and they supported me in ways I didn't expect. I'll be forever grateful to Carol and all the crew of *RPA*. They are amazing people for doing the job that they do, but also for having supported me the way they did. I'll never forget it.

Those weeks were some of the longest of my life.

Once we found out it had spread to my groin, I remember coming home and gathering everyone around the back table. It was meant to host family dinners and quiet moments, with the kids playing in the background. Instead, that table became the setting for one of the hardest conversations I've ever had to have.

I sat there with my family, trying to keep it together as I told them the news. 'It's spread,' I said, and the words just hung in the air between us. My mum started crying, her face crumpling. Dad just got up and left. He didn't say anything, didn't look back, just disappeared. At the time, I was so confused. I thought, *I just told you I've got bloody cancer, and it's spread. Why would you leave?*

But later, I realised it wasn't because he didn't care, it was because he did. My dad's from that old-school era – he's a stiff-upper-lip, 'she'll be right' kind of guy. He's not one for showing emotion – not in front of me, at least. I'm pretty sure he went round the corner somewhere to let it all out. That was just his way of coping. Mum, on the other hand, tried to put on a brave face for me. 'You'll be right, son,' she said, over and over. 'I've got a good feeling about this. You're strong, you'll get through it.'

She's always been like that. Even now, every time I've had scan results or bad news, she's there with her unshakable optimism, saying, 'You'll be fine, you'll be fine.' In a way, it helped. It was something to cling to, even if I didn't fully believe it myself.

The kids were too young to really understand what was happening. Jayden was just a little boy at the time and Shaylee was even younger. Janine, though, was my rock through it all. She was the one I turned to with all my questions, the one who kept me grounded when my thoughts spiralled.

Physically, I felt fine, at least at first. I had no symptoms, no pain. It was the mental toll that was wearing me down. I kept replaying the doctor's words in my head: 'It could be in your liver, lungs or brain.' Some people told me later that they thought he'd been too blunt. But I think he was just being honest, laying it all out there. Having information delivered in such a blunt way was always a lot to take in. There were stats, survival rates, surgical plans and all this medical language flying at me. I was always trying to listen, trying to process it the best I could, but it was as if my brain just tapped out at certain points. It was too much.

But once I got to know Doctor Quinn and his team more, I understood why they always gave it to me straight. That's just how it had to be done. Back then, melanoma was pretty much a death sentence. It didn't respond to treatment the way it can now. There were no miracle drugs, no promising trials on the horizon – it all just came down to facing the hard facts. So they didn't sugar-coat anything, and looking back, I'm glad they didn't. As hard as it was to hear in the moment, I needed to know exactly what I was facing.

For those two weeks, I walked around in a daze, convinced I was already dying. Every little ache or twinge was like proof that the cancer was spreading further. Ahead of my next operation, I was booked in for a full-body CT scan to assess if the cancer had spread further to my other organs. By the time it came around, I was a mess. The waiting was the worst part. I hated waiting for results, waiting for answers. It felt like I was waiting to find out if my life was already over.

•

The scan was booked for the day before my big operation, and the *RPA* crew was with me every step of the way. I tried to act composed for the cameras, but inside, I was an absolute mess. Before I knew it, I was being prepped for radioactive imaging. The idea of being scanned head to toe for hidden tumours, being told the results could change everything, was a lot to take in.

'CT', I learned, stands for 'computed tomography'. The scan takes lots of detailed X-rays of your whole body, your soft tissue and your organs, checking whether cancer has spread anywhere else. They inject you with this dye to make the contrast in the pictures clearer. You lie there for what feels like an age while this big machine circles you, scanning every inch of your body. It's completely painless, but mentally it's a roller-coaster. It was one of the more confronting moments in the whole process because it wasn't just about the melanoma on my ankle anymore. It was about whether this thing had decided to bury deeper into my body.

I remember lying dead still in the machine, surrounded by hums and clicks, and thinking: *Why do I even need this? Is there something they haven't told me?* My brain kicked into overdrive. *What if it's already in my lungs? What if it's in my brain? What if it's everywhere and I'm just too late?*

They explained the processes calmly, clinically, but all I really heard was: 'We don't know yet. We can't tell you. You'll have to wait.'

The waiting was the hardest part. The uncertainty drove me crazy. I had no idea if the cancer had spread or if I still had a fighting chance. A psychologist came and offered to talk things through with me, but I shut them down. I didn't want to talk about my feelings. I didn't want mindfulness or breathing exercises. I wanted facts. I wanted to be told, straight up, if I was going to live or die. But no-one could tell me that. Not yet. That rattled me more than anything else.

The crew wanted the results revealed on camera, a nice dramatic moment to tie the story together. The filming was planned for the next day. But my nerves were shot; every worst-case scenario I'd read online was running through my brain on a loop. I needed to know what I was dealing with.

So, after the scan, I stayed in the radiology department, pacing the halls like a man possessed. 'Can I please just have the results now?' I asked anyone who would listen. 'I need to know I'm okay.' The wait was absolutely unbearable – every second felt like a lifetime. After about an hour and a half, the head radiologist came out with the news: 'Look, there's nothing there. I can't see anything. But you need to get the full results from your treating doctor.'

The relief hit me like a tidal wave. Without thinking, I hugged the radiologist. It wasn't a polite, restrained hug, either; it was the kind of embrace you give someone who's just saved your life. She laughed awkwardly, probably not used to patients reacting like that, but I didn't care. Finally, in that moment at least, it felt like everything was okay.

The *RPA* crew didn't get to film that conversation, even though they'd badly wanted to. The radiologist wouldn't allow it. I could tell they were disappointed – they'd wanted to get my raw emotional reaction on camera, but honestly, I didn't care. This was my life. It wasn't about TV scripts or dramatic reveals. It was about knowing that, for now, the cancer hadn't spread further.

That night, the crew put us up at the Rydges near the hospital. It was a long night – once again, I couldn't sleep. Even though I'd got good news from the radiologist, I couldn't stop worrying about the operation the next day. Despite the clear scans, there were still so many unknowns. What if the lymph nodes in my groin came back positive? What if the melanoma had already started spreading beyond that one node, but hadn't been found because the cells were too small to be picked up on a scan? I couldn't let myself relax, not yet. There was always something else to worry about.

The next morning, Doctor Quinn confirmed the scan results on camera. 'You're all clear,' he said. 'The scans came back clean. But there's still concern about the lymph nodes in your groin.' His words felt like a double-edged sword. I was relieved, of course, that the cancer hadn't spread to any of my vital organs. But the uncertainty about the lymph nodes still hung over me.

Doctor Quinn explained that during the operation, as well as removing the lymph nodes, they'd also be taking out a big chunk of skin from my groin and stomach to test. It all needed to come back clear – the lymph nodes, the skin sample, everything. One misstep, one bad result, and I'd be in trouble.

The operation was scheduled for 6.30 am – perfect for someone already running on the fumes of anxiety, as it meant less time for me to agonise over what might happen. I remember being wheeled into the sterile corridors of the operating theatre, but that's it. Beyond that, everything is a blur. As soon as the anaesthetic kicked in, I was gone.

•

When I came to, I was back in the ward. Janine and Shaylee were sitting beside me, and seeing them immediately brought me comfort. They'd brought a card and a bright, cheerful 'Get Well Soon' balloon.

That second operation was brutal. They took the skin sample from my groin and stomach, and they removed almost every lymph node in my groin. I came out of that surgery with forty-four staples running from my stomach to my thigh. I found it hard to look at myself in the mirror after that. Looking at the scar for the first time stopped me cold. My body didn't look like mine anymore. The skin was swollen and bruised, stitched tight and shiny in places, sunken in others. I'd always been proud of keeping myself fit and strong. It felt like a cruel joke that wanting to look good was what had landed me here in the first place; now the guy I saw in the mirror was scarred and broken.

For years, the gym had been my escape, my way of feeling in control. I trained hard, lifted heavy and took care of myself, and suddenly that had all been ripped away. Even lying in the hospital bed was painful. My leg felt heavy and numb at the same time, like it belonged to someone else.

I found myself grieving the body I used to have, the strength I'd built and the sense of normality I'd lost. The physical toll was one thing, but the mental weight was just as heavy, if not heavier. I'd stare at those staples and think, *Is this me now? Is this what I'm going to look like forever?* It was the unknown that was haunting me – how much of a scar would be left, if I'd be able to train the same again or whether I'd even walk properly.

I'd been given strict instructions not to move. For five days, I was stuck in that hospital bed. The cut they'd made was massive, and I couldn't move my leg at all without a sharp reminder of what my body had just endured. I was on a morphine drip, and every few minutes, I'd press the button for another dose, just to dull the constant, throbbing pain.

I was still pretty out of it the first night, but every detail of the second night is carved into my memory – it's like it happened yesterday. Janine and Shaylee had gone home, the ward lights were dimmed so everyone could get some sleep, and this meant I was all alone with my thoughts. Everything hit me like a freight train, all at once. I was in the cancer ward. I was thirty-two years old, surrounded by patients much older than me, many of them fighting different types of cancer. I couldn't help feeling out of place, like I didn't belong there. But that was when I realised that, actually, I did. It was a tough thing to accept. Lying there, surrounded by older cancer patients, some of them terminal, it was impossible not to picture myself in their shoes.

The man across from me had advanced prostate cancer. He looked me dead in the eye and said, 'I don't have long to live.' The words were like a punch to the chest.

I couldn't stop thinking about Shaylee and Jayden, and about Janine and our unborn child. Shaylee and Jayden were still so little; Jayden was twelve and Shaylee was only ten. Way too young to lose a parent. I kept thinking, *They need their dad. I can't let them grow up with a memory instead of a father.* I didn't want to wind up as a photo on the wall, just someone they talked about at birthdays.

The awful realisation that cancer wasn't just something that happened to other and older people, that it was happening to me, *now*, and it could take me away from my family and the life we were still building, was more terrifying than anything they could've found on a scan. I lay there, dosed up on morphine, a drain snaking out of me, staring at the drip bags hanging overhead, and all I felt was fear. I wasn't just scared for myself; I was scared about what my absence would mean for the people I loved most. I was imagining their future, staring down my own mortality. I hated the idea that they might have to live with the impact of this disease long after I was gone.

It was as if all the emotions I'd been suppressing came crashing down at once, like the weight of everything I'd been trying to hold together finally came loose. I broke down, crying uncontrollably. I wasn't sobbing or making a scene; they were just quiet tears that wouldn't stop. The kind that come from deep down. They took me by surprise.

That was the first time I'd really cried in years. I'm not someone who cries easily. I grew up thinking strength meant always pushing through, holding it all in. But lying there in that hospital bed, none of that mattered. I cried because I was scared, and I felt helpless. I didn't know what tomorrow was going to bring.

On top of the physical pain, the feeling of vulnerability was overwhelming. I hated not knowing what would happen next. My body was broken, and my mind was spiralling into every dark possibility I could think of. I felt like a little kid, desperately wanting someone to tell me everything would be okay. But no-one could promise me that.

I was in a lot of pain during those five days. The staples made every movement agony, and the tube draining blood from my leg was a constant reminder of everything that was going on in my body. Basic tasks turned into massive challenges. I remember needing to use a bedpan. A nurse stood by the bed, waiting while I awkwardly did what I had to do. It was humiliating, but there was no other option. I couldn't get up, let alone move around. I was completely trapped in that bed.

But the physical discomfort wasn't the worst part – it was the mental toll. I'd ask the nurses, 'Do you think I'll be okay? What are the chances?' Unfortunately, although they were lovely, the nurses couldn't give me that reassurance. 'You'll have to wait for your doctor,' they'd tell me, gently but firmly. It was protocol, of course; they weren't allowed to speculate. Through everything, the nurses were absolutely amazing, working around the clock to look after me. I'll always have massive respect for the work nurses do and the care they show. They are amazing humans.

I spent hours replaying every scenario I'd read online. Google had been both a blessing and a curse – it connected me with people's stories, but not many of those stories had happy endings. I heard tales of loss, of treatments failing, of people succumbing to the disease. I couldn't find a single person who said, 'I had what you had and look at me – I'm still here five, ten years later.' That lack of hope, that absence of connection, was devastating.

That's when I realised how much of a difference it would have made to have someone there, a survivor, someone who'd been through it and come out the other side. Just to hear someone say, 'I've been where you are, and you're going to get through this,' would have been a lifeline. But there was no-one. Just me stuck in a hospital bed, in pain and drowning in the fear that I wasn't going to make it.

Looking back now, I can see that's part of why I became so passionate about support and advocacy. I don't want anyone else to feel the way I did – alone, scared and uncertain. But in that moment, I wasn't thinking about the future. I was just trying to get through the night. If someone who had beaten melanoma had visited me during those dark times, it would have made such a difference.

My five days in hospital seemed to drag on forever, but I found small ways to distract myself. Visitors came and went, breaking up the days, and my family made regular appearances, always trying to lift my spirits. One of my comforts during my hospital stay was reading *Big League* and *Rugby League Week* magazines, the same ones I'd loved when I was a kid. Flipping through those magazines gave me a little bit of normality and took me back to my childhood. I read articles about mates who had gone on to play professional footy, feeling a pang of nostalgia. It was bittersweet, but I was proud of my mates. Those magazines and the visits from my loved ones were a welcome distraction, and a helpful reminder that life still existed beyond those hospital walls, even if it felt far away.

It struck me as strange, even kind of funny, that at thirty-two years old, lying in a hospital bed, I was reading the same magazines I'd loved as a boy. But when you're surrounded by the heaviness of cancer, you cling to the things that remind you of who you are – not just a patient, but a person.

Still, it wasn't easy to stay positive during those days. I didn't feel brave; I just knew I had to keep going. Janine was my rock. She never faltered, even when I was falling apart. Sitting beside me, holding my hand, she'd say, 'Jay, it's going to be fine. It's just a tiny, little spot in one lymph node. If it had spread more, we'd know. This is manageable.' She broke down all the medical jargon into reassuring facts, which I clung to, repeating them until I started to believe her.

Her support during those dark days wasn't just comforting – it was next level. She was only in her twenties, but the way she handled everything that got thrown at us still blows me away. She's a machine when it comes to that kind of pressure. Nothing rattles her too much. She just gets on with it, staying grounded, sticking to the facts and doing what needs to be done with no complaints and no fuss. And this was no different.

Every morning, she'd be there first thing, walking into that hospital room with a quiet strength that held me together more than she probably realised. She didn't leave until late at night, staying by my side through the painful moments, the long silences and scarier conversations. Always making sure I was comfortable, that I had everything I needed. Even though she was pregnant, even though her body was going through its own massive changes, even though she must've been exhausted and scared herself, she just kept showing up.

Without her, I don't know how I would have got through it. When it came time for her to leave each night, I felt the fear starting to claw at me. I'd feel it rising the minute she stood up to say goodbye. I didn't want her to see it, but the truth was, I was terrified of being alone at night. The dark made everything heavier. It was when the overthinking kicked in, the fear, the stats, the what-ifs. And when she left, that's when I'd have to face it all on my own.

But no matter how scared I was, I always knew she'd be back the next morning. That thought kept me going. In the middle of all that fear and uncertainty, Janine was my anchor. She still is.

10

LIFE IN LIMBO

Waiting for the results after that second surgery was torture. I struggled through another week of uncertainty, trying to hold it together emotionally while my body healed. Those days blurred together, each one stretching on endlessly as I counted down to the next appointment, when I'd finally get more answers. But as the fifth day approached, I started to sense a shift. Janine had visited earlier and brought some reassurance. She told me, 'I spoke to the doctor, and he said the operation went well.' Those words gave me a sliver of hope.

When the time finally came, I walked into the room, once again surrounded by cameras. As the crew set me up with microphones, the atmosphere was noticeably different. Everyone seemed brighter, lighter, chatting easily. I leaned over to Janine and said, 'I think it's going to be alright. They're all chirpy today.'

When the doctor finally walked in, the vibe shifted again. 'It's all clear,' he said with a smile. 'Just stay away from solariums and tanning from now on.' His words hit me like a tidal wave of relief. The crushing fear that had loomed over me for months lifted in an instant. I turned to Janine, pulled her into a hug and just let myself breathe. It was over, for now, at least.

That day felt surreal. This time, when we drove home from the hospital, everything seemed different. It was like stepping out of a nightmare and into a bright, sunny day. For the first time in months, I felt free – the relief was overwhelming. The fear of dying, the endless appointments, the constant googling of symptoms and survival rates – all of it seemed to fade into the background. I was told I wouldn't need to come back for another three months. Three whole months! After living from week to week, that felt like a gift.

As we drove, my thoughts began to wander beyond the fact that I'd survived. I was hit with the realisation that

I'd been given another chance. Janine and I could finally start planning our wedding in earnest, something we'd been holding off on while we waited for more tests and more results. But alongside those thoughts about my own life, other thoughts started to creep in. What about all the others out there who were still tanning, with no idea of the risks? I couldn't shake the image of someone lying in a solarium, unknowingly heading down the same path I'd just fought so hard to escape. That thought stuck with me; I couldn't let it go. I had to do something.

•

After the operation, Doctor Quinn scheduled my three-month check-up. I couldn't believe I'd get to enjoy three months without constant appointments and tests, no waiting rooms, no constant dread. He explained how it would work: I'd head to RPA, get my blood tests done, then go for scans, and finally go and see him to get the results.

Those follow-ups became routine, a part of my life that I never really got used to, though there was no getting around them. Doctor Quinn would see me every six months. He'd check that the staples had healed properly and make sure my lymph nodes hadn't swollen. He'd press his hand under my armpit, feeling around for any irregularities. 'Nine times out of ten, it's the patient who finds a lump, not the doctor,' he'd say. Those words stayed with me. After that, every week in the shower, I'd do the same checks, running my hands over my body, feeling for anything unusual. It was like a ritual, one I dreaded but knew I couldn't neglect.

Over time, Doctor Quinn became more than just a medical professional to me – he was more like my mentor. In later years, I started working at the Melanoma Institute Australia, where he was based, and we formed a bond. I trusted him completely, and he always made time to listen to my concerns. I'd drop into his office and say, 'Mate, is this anything to worry about? I need you to help me out.' He was always happy to provide reassurance or guidance.

In 2018, Doctor Quinn passed away. The news hit me hard. He'd been at my house just a month before for a family barbecue. Losing him was devastating. He had saved my life and supported me through the darkest period of it. I'll always remember him not just as my doctor, but as someone who truly cared. He'd played such a key role in giving me the chance to keep going. I was truly honoured when his family asked me to speak at his funeral. I broke down a couple of times, but I know he would have been proud. His family came up to me afterwards and thanked me for sharing how Doctor Quinn cared about his patients.

Alongside Doctor Quinn, I was also under the care of Doctor Anne Hamilton, an oncologist at RPA, who I saw every three months. She was in charge of the scans, the blood tests, the imaging – all the deep dives into my health. Every visit to her felt like a gamble. I'd hold my breath, waiting for the results, terrified I was out of luck. But each time, when the tests were clear, I'd feel like I could breathe again – at least until the next one. Those three-month intervals were suffocating. It was a constant cycle of fear, relief and then fear again.

The next five years after my diagnosis became a routine of those three-monthly check-ins, each one a nerve-racking ordeal. Every three months, I'd go in for a blood test and a chest X-ray. Sitting in the waiting room, I'd always catch myself thinking, *Why can't I just be here for something simple?* A broken leg, a sprained wrist, anything but melanoma. Every step of the process was loaded with anxiety.

The X-ray itself was always the same. I'd stand there, holding on to the machine while they took the images. Then I had to wait outside the room while the radiologist checked the scans. I'd try to act casual, but usually I'd sneak a glance around the corner to try and get a glimpse of what they were looking at. Every single time, they'd come back, tell me to put my shirt on and say I could go.

That moment, those few words, felt like being handed a gift. *All clear.* I'd walk out of the room feeling a mix of relief and gratitude, but there was always the voice in the back of my mind whispering, *It's only for now.*

The relief would last about two months. For those eight weeks, I could live my life without the dark cloud of uncertainty hanging over me. But as soon as that third month approached, the anxiety would start to build again. By the time the next appointment rolled around, I'd be a bundle of nerves. Janine would always try to keep me grounded, telling me not to panic, that everything would be fine. I'd nod along, but it was hard to stop the worry from taking over.

Between check-ups, I'd spend hours obsessively googling, this time for stories of cancer coming back. Those stories were everywhere. Blogs, forums, medical sites – they all painted a grim picture. I'd read about recurrences, treatments that didn't work, lives cut short. Then there were the funeral notices. I'd scroll through them, searching for names and ages that matched mine. Each story chipped away at me.

I'd wake up in the middle of the night, my mind racing, and head straight for the computer. I'd sit there at two in the morning, reading the same stories I'd seen before, as if hoping for a different ending. But it was always the same:

tragedy after tragedy. I was torturing myself; I couldn't help it. The internet became both my refuge and my tormentor – I went there looking for answers, but only found more questions.

Those were some of the darkest nights. I was always bracing for the next bit of bad news, the next scan that might reveal something I couldn't fight. The fear was relentless, but it also became a driving force. I couldn't let this thing win, not without knowing I'd done everything I possibly could to beat it.

11

IN SICKNESS AND IN HEALTH

In the middle of everything, all the scans and procedures and time in hospital, Janine and I had still been planning our wedding. After the operations, we had decided to move it forward to May. Even though I'd been declared officially cancer-free, I was convinced I didn't have much time left. All the reading I'd done online and all the stories I'd consumed painted such a bleak picture. There was nothing positive or reassuring in anything I found, just stories of people losing their battles. That gave me a sense of urgency, a feeling that weighed heavily on both me and Janine. We wanted to make sure we didn't wait too long.

As always, Janine was the positive one through all of this. She'd try to reassure me, saying, 'Jay, the doctors have done their job. If there was more, they'd have caught it. You need to move on and live your life.' My dad, in his tough-love way, would say, 'Get on with it, son. Go back to work.' But I couldn't. Their words, while well-meaning, just didn't get through. I couldn't just flip a switch and move forward. I was trapped in my own fears, convinced I had maybe eight months, a year at best. I was convinced I was going to die, and nothing anyone said could change my mind.

Some people, I've noticed, are different: they're much more resilient. They accept that life is uncertain and keep moving forward regardless. But I was young back then, scared, and starved of information.

So we decided to get married as soon as possible, and set the date for 10 May. I thought, *Let's do it while I'm still here, before things get worse.* Every moment became incredibly emotional. I cried all the time. Everything felt overwhelming. Looking back, I realise I didn't have the kind of support I truly needed. It wasn't anyone's fault – those support systems just weren't available in those days. That sense of isolation really stayed with me. It's why I'm so passionate about running support groups now. I know exactly how terrifying it is to face something like melanoma without knowing anyone who gets what you're going through.

RPA came down and filmed the wedding for the show. It was surreal, really, being surrounded by cameras on what was such an intimate and emotional day. But at the time, I didn't care about the cameras or the audience. I was just focused on Janine, on our family and on making sure we got to have that moment together, no matter what the future held.

Janine and I decided to get married at Lagoon in Wollongong, a beautiful seafood restaurant where we'd had one of our first dates. It seemed fitting to go back there for our big day, and the setting was perfect: lush green lawns leading up to the water, a carpet rolled out for the ceremony.

Planning the wedding gave us something to focus on, something joyful to take our minds off our worries. It wasn't cheap, though – $40,000 for one day. Even now, that's a lot of money, but in 2008, it felt monumental.

While it wasn't the planning process we'd imagined, somehow it made the whole experience even more meaningful. As per usual, Janine was amazing throughout it all. She did the majority of the planning at four months pregnant, alongside her sister Jaclyn, my sister Chantal and both our families. It was a real team effort. I remember one day we had a specialist appointment in the morning, and afterward we headed to Parramatta. Janine went to try on wedding dresses, and I sat at a local cafe nearby, waiting for her with a green tea in hand. That's how we made it work, squeezing wedding prep in between doctor visits and hospital scans, making the most of every spare moment.

I took on a few jobs myself, organising the groomsmen, sorting out the cars and helping out with the reception. It felt good to be able to contribute, even in small ways, and to give myself a focus beyond my health.

It was all worth it in the end. The wedding day itself was magical. Everything went off without a hitch, and it felt like a real celebration of love, family and resilience. We had about 140 guests – a big wedding by any standard. Family, friends, everyone came together to celebrate with us, and the atmosphere was incredible. It was a chance to hit pause, take a deep breath and just enjoy the love and support we were surrounded by.

For me, the day was deeply emotional. While everyone else was celebrating, I couldn't fully let go of the fear that this could be one of my last moments with all these people I loved. In my speech, I probably waffled on a bit too long, but I couldn't help it. I wanted to soak in every second, to hold on to the precious time I had with my family and Janine. I was still convinced I was going to die, and that made every moment feel bittersweet. I made a point to speak to every single guest, to soak up the hugs, the laughter and the little moments. I didn't want to miss anything. Despite the bittersweet feeling, it was another milestone Janine and I had reached together.

We did go on a honeymoon, but honestly, the details are hazy now. I was still in the thick of treatments and medical appointments, and my mind was so consumed with worry. We ended up going to a resort in North Queensland for our honeymoon, and while we were there, I came down with a bad case of the flu. I booked in to see a local GP, just thinking I'd get some meds and be on my way. But when he looked over my notes and saw I'd recently been diagnosed with stage 3 melanoma, he said something that absolutely floored me. He looked me dead in the eye and said, 'Gee, that's a bad diagnosis. I want you to send me a Christmas card every year you're still here, because I don't like your chances.'

I walked out of that office in complete silence. When I told Janine what he'd said, she was gobsmacked and couldn't believe it. She wanted to march back in there and give him a piece of her mind, but instead, we just carried on with the honeymoon, trying not to let it ruin our time away. Still, those words haunted me for years. They cut deep, and for a long time, they added to the fear that was already sitting heavy on my chest.

We've been back to the area a few times since, and I've actually tried to find that GP – not to confront him, but just to say, 'Hey mate, I'm still here.' I wanted him to see that I made it through, and to maybe think twice before speaking so bluntly to someone else facing what I was facing. A little hope goes a long way.

•

Being married and knowing we had a baby on the way played a big part in driving me forward. I wanted to do everything I could to ensure I was around for my family. Jaxon was born later that year, in November, a bright spot in what felt like such a dark time. His arrival brought us both joy and a renewed sense of purpose.

It was around that same time that our first *RPA* episode aired, months after everything had happened in real life, but long before I was 'recovered' mentally. By then, Janine and I were eager to sit down and watch it all back. It was such a surreal experience. I knew the cameras had been there documenting every step, but seeing it on TV, watching myself go through such a life-changing experience, was something else entirely.

Watching the episode of *RPA* for the first time was surreal. There I was, holding my tiny newborn son in my arms, while on screen, this past version of me was fighting for his life. The contrast between what I was watching and what I was living couldn't have been starker. I was in this joyful, hopeful chapter of my life, but the show pulled me straight back into all that fear and fragility.

Seeing myself pale, gaunt and emotionally raw hit harder than I expected. Watching it was like reliving it through someone else's eyes. The cameras had captured so much more than just the procedures. They'd caught the silences, the hesitation in my voice, the look in my eyes when the fear crept in. It was accurate – in some ways, almost too accurate. When I'd been going through it, the fear and uncertainty had drowned out everything else. At the time, I couldn't have cared less if the footage ended up on national TV. All I wanted was hope and a chance to keep going. But watching it months later brought memories flooding back that I'd tried to bury. The sounds of the hospital, the way Janine would grip my hand just before a procedure, the anxious feeling in my stomach when the doctor walked into the room to give me my test results.

Family and friends tuned in to watch, too, and suddenly, people who had only seen the surface of what we'd been through were hit with the reality of it all. I got messages from people who were shocked, emotional, even inspired. Some hadn't realised just how close I'd come to the edge.

My parents found it hard to watch – I think seeing it all unfold on screen made it more real for them in hindsight.

It felt like the ratings must've been through the roof because so many people reached out to us after the show aired. In the lead-up to the first episode airing, I'd been featured pretty heavily in the previews. The network had cut together some dramatic teasers, as TV producers do, and they made it look like my life was hanging in the balance. That kind of thing draws viewers in, I get it. But what I didn't expect was the flood of messages from people genuinely worried I hadn't made it through. Some of them were just checking in; others flat-out asked if I was still alive.

Reading those messages was confronting, to say the least. I knew the show was powerful and raw, but seeing how many people thought I might be gone really rattled me. It was surreal to be watching it unfold on TV with everyone else, knowing I was still fighting, still here. This was my life, my fight, on display for everyone to see.

It was the first time I truly understood the power of sharing my story. Sure, it was confronting, but it also planted the seed: maybe this could help others. Maybe, by showing how awful melanoma really is, we could stop someone else from going through the same thing.

12

CANCER-FREE BUT NOT FREE YET

In the months following the operation, my anxiety didn't let up. Planning the wedding gave us something happy to focus on for a while, but I was still living in fear of the cancer rearing its ugly head again. I was desperate to do anything I could to keep it at bay.

In one of our appointments, Doctor Hamilton introduced me to something called interferon treatment, a form of immunotherapy to help ensure the cancer didn't come back. Interferon's a funny one. It's not like chemo, which directly attacks the cancer cells – it's more like giving your immune system a megaphone and saying,

'Oi, wake up! There's danger in here, do something about it!' Interferon is a protein your body already makes in small amounts when you're sick, like when you've got a virus. But in treatment, they give it to you in high doses, which sends your immune system into overdrive, hunting down anything that looks even slightly off (like rogue cancer cells that might've slipped through the cracks).

Back then, interferon seemed like the only option available for someone in my position, who had been given the all-clear but had a high risk of the cancer reappearing. It wasn't perfect – the side effects were rough, and it didn't work for everyone – but it gave you a fighting chance. These days, they've got more advanced immunotherapies that target things more precisely, but interferon was the best shot we had back then. Was it safe? Yeah, relatively. But it pushed your body hard, resulting in fevers, fatigue and big hits to your mood. Still, when your life is on the line, you cop it and keep going.

Doctor Hamilton had talked about it for weeks, explaining the potential benefits and risks, laying out what it might mean for my recovery. But in the end, it turned out it wasn't up to her to decide if I'd have the treatment – it was up to a computer program, which would determine whether I'd receive the treatment or simply be placed under observation.

When the decision finally came through, it felt like the air had been knocked out of me. Observation. That was it. No treatment, just a wait-and-see approach. I couldn't believe it. After everything, after all the build-up, everything Doctor Hamilton had told me about how interferon might help, they weren't going to give it to me. I went home that night and started googling everything I could find about interferon. I didn't want to be a statistic, and I wasn't just going to sit around while cancer decided my fate.

Doctor Hamilton had talked up the treatment, warning me about the potential side effects and explaining how it might help. So when I was told that some computer algorithm had determined I wasn't eligible, I was furious. How could my life be in the hands of a decision made by a computer? I wasn't just a statistic or some data entered into a machine. My life was worth more than that. I refused to accept it.

So I took matters into my own hands. I called hospitals all across the country, telling them my story and asking for options. I wasn't going to let this go. Most of the responses were sympathetic but unhelpful, but finally, one call to Westmead Hospital changed everything. The woman on the other end of the line said: 'It's your life. If you want the treatment, fight for it. Ask to be referred.' That was all the encouragement I needed. I went back to my oncologist, laid out what I'd learned and insisted on being referred to Westmead.

Doctor Hamilton seemed surprised, even a little taken aback. 'Who have you been talking to?' she asked. I explained my calls and what I'd learned, and to her credit, she didn't try to stop me. She was a lovely human. Instead, she referred me to Professor Rick Kefford at Westmead, one of the world's leading oncologists at the time. Professor Kefford agreed to take me on, and to administer the interferon.

Even after securing the interferon treatment, I still didn't feel like I could take it easy. After Doctor Quinn had declared me cancer-free, everyone around me was urging me to get back to normal life, to return to work, to move on. But for me, it wasn't that simple. The word 'cancer-free' seemed like a fragile promise, one that could shatter at any moment. I couldn't shake the fear that the cancer would come back. The interferon treatment was like my insurance policy. I needed to know I'd done everything in my power to keep the cancer away. I didn't want to have any regrets or what-ifs.

At the end of May, just after our wedding, I started treatment. It was gruelling. I went to Westmead every day for three weeks to receive the interferon intravenously. Each session only took about twenty minutes, but mentally, it felt like hours. Sitting in the cancer ward, surrounded by people far sicker than me, many of them bald, pale and frail, it was impossible not to feel the weight of it all. It was a constant reminder of how close I'd come to being in their shoes.

On the very first day of treatment, I made a rookie mistake. I've always loved chilli, and that day, before heading to Westmead Hospital, I treated myself to a spicy meal. It didn't even cross my mind that this might complicate things. The treatment itself was straightforward, and I left the hospital thinking everything was fine.

But later that night, I woke up in excruciating pain – it felt like my chest was about to explode. It was terrifying. Janine called an ambulance, and before I knew it, I was rushed to Campbelltown Hospital. The doctors were alarmed – my heart rate was skyrocketing and my levels were all over the place. After some investigation, they finally worked out that the chilli I'd eaten earlier had interacted with the treatment, causing severe heartburn and other complications. It could have killed me. They adjusted my dosage and gave me strict instructions: no more chilli, ever.

The high-dose interferon was intense, pushing my body to its limits. I'd have the treatment in the morning, and by late afternoon, I'd be gearing up to do it all over again the next day. My joints ached constantly, my energy levels were at rock-bottom, and I felt like a zombie most of the time.

Those days of treatment were some of the hardest I've ever endured. I didn't lose my hair entirely, but it thinned out noticeably, and the weight just fell off me. I still cringe looking at photos of myself from that time. They're a stark reminder of how much my body was put through.

The treatment itself wasn't instant. You'd go in, have it administered intravenously, and for a couple of hours, you'd feel fine, almost normal. But then, like clockwork, it would hit you, this tidal wave of exhaustion and discomfort. It was like being slammed with the worst cold you could imagine. My head would be foggy, my body aching, and I'd just sit around, unable to do anything; I just had to wait for it to pass.

The mornings were tough, but the nights were worse. By the time I woke up the next day, the heaviness from the treatment would have eased just enough for me to make it through another round.

Again, Janine was my rock through all of it. She'd drive me to Westmead and back, balancing everything else in her life while making sure I had what I needed. On the days she was working, though, she couldn't come with me. I'd drive myself in for treatment on those days, even though I probably shouldn't have.

By the third week of the treatment, I had lost seven kilograms. My appetite was non-existent except for one peculiar craving: Big Macs. They were the only thing I could stomach. Every day after treatment, I'd swing by McDonald's.

By the end of that third week, my liver was under massive stress. The amount of alanine transaminase (an enzyme that we normally have pretty low levels of in our blood) in my body had skyrocketed to almost twenty times the safe level. Professor Kefford gave me a choice: I could wait another week for my liver to recover and then continue, or we could stop the treatment altogether. 'I think it's done enough,' he said, and I agreed.

The interferon treatment felt like my best shot at securing a future. I thought, *If I can just get through this, I'll be safe. I can put it all behind me.* That was the goal: survive the treatment, eliminate any trace of cancer and move on.

Looking back, I'm glad I fought for the treatment. It was my decision, my choice, and that mattered to me. It reminded me that even in the face of something as overwhelming as cancer, I still had some control. That experience taught me that when it comes to your own life, you have to be your own advocate. No-one can fight for you like you can fight for yourself.

13

ONE STEP AT A TIME

In the months after the operations, I leaned on anyone who would listen. A nurse at RPA, Penny, became my go-to whenever I felt that familiar knot of fear in my chest. If I woke up with a twinge in my groin or a sudden ache, I'd jump in the car and make the ninety-minute drive to her clinic. 'Penny, is this normal? Is it something I should worry about?'

And every time, she'd reassure me. 'You're fine, Jay. Go home. You're doing okay.' Those words kept me sane, even if they only calmed my panic for a little while.

Eventually, Penny referred me to a psychologist at RPA. Angela became a lifeline. She helped me untangle the chaos in my head, giving me tools to navigate the thoughts and fears that were overwhelming me. Sometimes Janine would join me, and Angela helped us as a couple, showing us how to cope together. Even now, I check in with her every six months or so. Those sessions were a turning point, a chance to regain some control and start putting one foot in front of the other. I owe a lot to Angela. She is an amazing human.

At the time, I wasn't working. I couldn't. Mentally, I just still wasn't there. I'd thought I'd be off work for a few weeks, maybe a month at most. But those weeks turned into months, and in the end, I was away from work for fourteen months. It wasn't just the physical recovery; it was the emotional toll. I was consumed by fear, convinced that the cancer was lying in wait, ready to resurface. Every three months for five years, I went through the same cycle: scans, blood tests and the agonising wait for results. It was like living in a constant state of limbo, never knowing if or when the next blow would come.

Around the ninth or tenth month post-operation, my aunt suggested I call the Cancer Council helpline. I'd never thought of doing that, but I was desperate. I called, and they told me about a generic cancer support group that was being run in Sydney. I decided to go. Meeting other people who had been through cancer was key in helping me realise that I wasn't alone.

It still took nearly twelve months for me to let myself believe the melanoma might not come back. That year was one of the hardest of my life, but those moments, talking to Angela, leaning on Janine and connecting with others who understood, helped me begin to heal.

Meeting other people who had been through the same battle was like finding salvation. Hearing their stories gave me a little spark of hope that maybe, just maybe, I could move past this. Up until then, I'd felt like I was staring down this impossible monster on my own, and that death was the only possible outcome. But sitting in that support group and hearing people share their stories, I started to believe I could beat this thing. That first meeting opened a door I hadn't even known was there.

At one of those sessions, I met Lisa and Herman, two great people who had come down from Queensland. Herman had gone through the same ordeal as me a few years earlier. 'I had what you had,' he told me, 'and I'm still here.' That simple sentence hit me like a jolt of electricity. Herman became one of my best mates. He was like my mentor, showing me the ropes of how to run a support group. Together, we got our own Sydney cancer support group off the ground. Herman gave me the confidence to help others.

We held our first support group meeting in an office boardroom at Coates in Liverpool. Another survivor, Harry, generously let us use the space in an act of kindness that meant the world to us. We put the word out through a local newspaper ad and an online melanoma chat group, not knowing if anyone would even show up. But that night, around nine people walked through the door, and honestly, it changed my world.

For the first time, I wasn't alone in this. I met others who were battling melanoma, just like me. There were also people who'd lost someone – husbands, wives, kids – and they were there not just to grieve but to support the rest of us. Just selfless humans showing up for others, even in their own pain. My kind of people. Well . . . my *new* kind of people. I never pictured myself as the support group type, but when your life gets flipped upside down, you do whatever you can to just get through each day.

The friendships I formed in those early meetings were deep and lasting. But with that connection came heart-break. Many of the people I met didn't make it – back then, treatments were limited. In those first few years, it felt like every few months I was saying goodbye to someone.

When I look back now, I realise it's been years since I've been to a funeral for someone lost to melanoma. Treatments have come a long way, thankfully. But those early years were brutal, and I carry those losses with me always.

Despite his role in demonstrating there was life after melanoma, and in one of the most ironically cruel twists in my life, Herman passed away in 2014 when his melanoma came back. I'll always remember the lessons he taught me. He was a true champion.

The Liverpool support group became a key part of my recovery. It was about sharing experiences but it was also about building something better. We realised that the system wasn't going to support us the way we needed to be supported, so we decided to create a support network for people who felt just as lost as we once did. While we were navigating the maze ourselves, we made a path for others to follow.

Through that group, I also met James Economides. Just six months before our first meeting, James had lost his twenty-year-old son, Michael, to melanoma. Despite his own grief, James came to that group ready to help others. He drove almost two hours to be there. The loss of his son was devastating; there's no other way to put it. But instead of focusing on his own pain, James poured his energy into supporting people like me. He didn't want anyone to feel scared or alone. His strength, knowledge and generosity were incredible. He and I have been close mates ever since.

James and I went on to co-found the Melanoma March, which the Melanoma Institute Australia still runs today. It's raised millions for melanoma research, something we never could've imagined back when it all began. We started it because we wanted to give people hope. At the time, there wasn't much out there for melanoma patients or their families. So, in 2012, we launched the first Melanoma March in Manly, to raise funds and awareness, and to show people they weren't alone in this fight.

James has been by my side through every fundraising walk since. He's not just a mate but someone I trust completely. Every new idea I've had over the years, I've run past him first. He's honest with me; he'll tell me straight if something won't work, or he'll just sit and listen as I throw ideas around.

James often talks about his son, who passed away from melanoma. I've heard those stories so many times I've lost count, and every time, he sheds a tear. Once, I said to him, 'Mate, you know you've told me this story a few times,' and he just smiled and said, 'Yeah, but you always listen.'

Giving someone space to share their story with someone who truly understands what they're going through is what those early days of support groups were all about for me: compassion, connection and a determination to make sure no-one ever felt alone.

•

Angela remained a constant through that period. Some weeks, I'd see her twice, on Monday and again on Friday. She was patient and kind, and she listened in a way that made me feel truly heard. Angela helped me untangle the fears that had taken over my mind. All the scans, the treatments, the waiting, it was all so overwhelming, but she gave me the tools to navigate it all.

That year wasn't just about emotional recovery; it changed my physical health routine, too. I threw myself into researching everything I could about melanoma, nutrition and boosting my immune system. One story I found online really stuck with me. It was about a man with inoperable tumours who drank carrot juice every day for months. His tumours shrank. That story lit a fire under me.

I realised we had a juicer sitting in the cupboard, still in its box. I pulled it out and started juicing carrots like a man on a mission. Every day, I'd juice a kilo, sometimes two. I added green apples, too, because I read they were also great for your immune system. It became a ritual: juice in the morning and juice before bed. I told myself the vitamins and nutrients were working while I slept, helping my body get strong.

At one point, my skin started turning orange. I had to laugh – I'd traded sunbeds for carrot juice, and now I didn't need to tan anymore. But I kept going. For almost four solid years, I drank juice nearly every day. It was more about the mental benefits than anything else. I truly believed it was helping me, and that belief gave me strength. Whether it was true or not, it gave me something to hold on to, something I could do for myself. And in the middle of all that chaos and fear, it gave me a small sense of control.

But all around me, people in the support group were losing their battles. I went to so many funerals, and every one of them hit hard. Some of these people had been diagnosed with less aggressive cases than mine, yet they were gone. And here I was, still standing. It was impossible to wrap my head around sometimes, how unfair and random cancer could be.

Throughout that year of recovery, my support network became a huge factor in how I tackled the mental and physical challenges. My parents, in particular, were both amazing in their own unique ways. My dad, being old-school, approached things with a tough-love mentality. 'Come on, mate, you've got to get on with it,' he'd say. At first it frustrated me, because I felt like he didn't fully understand what I was going through. But I knew that underneath it all, he cared deeply. That's just his way. My mum, on the other hand, was the emotional cornerstone. She was always the one checking in, asking about every scan and test. 'How'd you go, son?' she'd ask, and then relay the news to my dad. She never wavered in her encouragement. 'Just do what you've got to do, son. We're here. Keep going, you'll be alright.' Her belief in me kept me grounded, and it still does today.

Friends were a different story. Most were supportive, and their kindness meant a lot. But I did lose a couple of mates during that time. These were the guys I used to go to the pub with. They just didn't get the changes I was making. For them, it was simple: 'Toughen up, mate. You're over it. Come and have a drink and move on.' But I wasn't over it. I couldn't be. I wasn't the same person anymore, and I had no interest in going back to the life I'd had before. Eventually, I had to distance myself from them. It wasn't easy, but it was necessary. Thankfully, most understood and are still my mates today, but they know melanoma completely changed me.

I made a few major lifestyle changes during this time. I cut out beer completely, which had been a big part of those old social habits. I'd read that red wine, in moderation, could be good for you, so I allowed myself the occasional glass, maybe two or three a week, but that was it. Beer was gone for good. My focus shifted completely to doing everything I could to strengthen my immune system. I wanted to give myself the best possible chance of staying healthy.

Fitness had always been a part of my life, even before cancer turned everything upside down. Once again, I started exercising regularly. After they removed all the lymph nodes from my groin, my leg began to swell and I discovered that I'd developed lymphoedema in my left leg, a fluid build-up because the lymphatic system wasn't draining properly anymore. I saw a therapist who specialised in lymphatic drainage, a process that helps move fluid out of the affected area and toward the heart. It's incredible how it works, just through massage. They even taught Janine how to do it at home, and she became an expert. It really helped me manage the swelling. Swimming also helped – the gentle movement and water pressure work together to encourage drainage without putting stress on your joints, kind of like a natural massage. I wasn't smashing out laps like a champion, but even just floating or slow freestyle helped keep the swelling down and gave me a sense of control over my recovery.

In addition to swimming, I incorporated light weights and bodyweight exercises into my routine. I've always had weights at home, so I started doing everything, chin-ups, bicep curls and squats, though the squats had to be light because of my leg. Push-ups and lunges became staples as well. Exercise gave me a greater sense of control, a way to channel my energy and frustration into something productive. It wasn't just about improving my physical health; it was about proving to myself that I was still capable. Through this work, I started to rebuild my life, one step – or one rep – at a time.

These small but consistent efforts formed the backbone of my recovery. They gave me purpose, and a way to fight back against the fear that still loomed large in my mind. Bit by bit, I was carving out a new path, one that was healthier, more intentional and focused on what really mattered. It was a slow process, but every day, I felt a little bit stronger, physically, mentally and emotionally.

•

Returning to work after more than a year away was a challenge on so many levels. On one hand, there was a part of me that wanted to feel normal again, to have some sense of routine and purpose. But on the other hand, I was still consumed by fear. I was worried about how my leg would cope with the physical demands of the work and scared of spending hours on end isolated with my own thoughts in the cab of a truck. The jolts in my leg whenever I jumped out of the truck were a constant reminder of what I'd been through, and they made me worry that I was pushing myself too hard physically.

Mentally, it was even tougher. My job as a truck driver used to be straightforward: load up at six in the morning, hit the road and be back at the depot around 5.30. But now, sitting alone in that truck all day was unbearable. My mind would race, obsessing over whether the cancer was coming back. I kept asking myself, 'Why am I sitting in this truck, wasting time, when I could be with my family or making a difference?' My priorities had shifted, and what once felt like a stable routine now seemed like a prison.

Even the camaraderie at work wasn't the same anymore. The casual banter about weekends and sports that I used to enjoy now felt hollow. I just couldn't make small talk anymore – I couldn't pretend to care about those trivial things. My perspective on life had completely changed. I didn't want to talk about football scores; I wanted to change the world. I realised I couldn't keep doing that job. I decided it was time for me to move on: I needed to focus on something bigger, something meaningful.

14

BUILDING COMMUNITY

Life was hectic around this time. Janine and I were busy with our new baby, Jaxon, and I was regularly attending support groups. Soon, I was organising my own group meetings in Sydney, Sutherland and Wollongong. We'd advertise the meetings in local papers, inviting anyone who was dealing with melanoma to come along. It was grassroots, but it worked. People started showing up and sharing their stories. There was comfort in discovering that they weren't alone.

These meetings quickly became a cornerstone of my new life. They became a lifeline, a way to share experiences, learn and connect with others facing similar battles. They gave me a sense of purpose. At last, I was surrounded by a community of people who understood what I was going through. I knew it was about offering support to others, but it was about healing myself, too. I realised that by helping others navigate their journeys with melanoma, I was also finding my own path forward.

By 2009, my life seemed to be spinning in a million directions at once. I threw myself into advocacy and support work. I worked with Herman to set up more melanoma-specific support groups, and started laying the groundwork for the campaign to ban sunbeds. It was a lot to take on, but it felt like every day mattered. That fear I'd been carrying wouldn't ease up – as though I was racing against time to get things done and make an impact in case my next scan up-ended everything.

We held our first melanoma-specific meeting at the San Hospital in Wahroonga. That first day, sixty per cent of the people who showed up weren't melanoma patients themselves. They were family members who had lost loved ones to the disease and were looking for a way to channel their grief. Hearing their stories and seeing the connections form between these people as they shared their pain was incredible. Some of them are still close friends of mine today. The bonds you form in moments like those go beyond words, and they last a lifetime.

Around the same time, I started volunteering at RPA. I really wanted to find a way to give back and speak to other people were going through the same thing I had. When I talked to Angela about it, she made it all happen for me and connected me with the team at RPA. It was an opportunity to help people who were in the same place I'd been in just a year earlier, scared, uncertain and desperate for reassurance. I'd walk the wards delivering tea and biscuits, and I always kept an eye out for the colour-coding of the writing on the patient boards – green meant a patient had melanoma. Those were the rooms I gravitated toward. I'd introduce myself and let them know I'd been in their shoes. Not everyone wanted to talk, and that was fine. But for those who did, it felt like that conversation helped ease some of their fear, even just a little.

I'll never forget one particular woman I met during those rounds. She had tumours visibly protruding from her body, and told me she only had a couple of weeks to live. She was sad, but she was happy to chat. I ended up visiting her regularly until she passed. The experience was both heartbreaking and terrifying. I couldn't help wondering, *Is that going to be me someday?* The fear was almost paralysing, but it also pushed me to keep going back. Even when I found myself thinking, *I can't do this anymore,* I'd still go back the following week. There was something about those connections, however brief, that felt important – not just for them, but for me as well. Giving back was very important to me. After all, that hospital saved my life.

My fear was always just beneath the surface. It was like a constant shadow, whispering, 'What if your next scan isn't clear?' That fear drove me to cram as much as I could into every day. I didn't want to waste a second. Whether it was organising support groups or volunteering on the wards, I was relentless. But it wasn't easy.

Every three months, the routine was the same: I'd get a scan, hold my breath while I waited for the results, then use the brief relief of being given the all-clear to push even harder. It wasn't sustainable, but at the time, it felt like the only way to live.

Looking back, it's clear how much that fear shaped me. It wasn't just about surviving anymore; it was about making the most of the time I'd been given. That constant back-and-forth between relief and fear drove me to channel everything into advocacy and support work. I was determined to turn my fear into something meaningful.

Suddenly, I was in tune with emotions I hadn't even known I had. Janine noticed it, too. We'd be sitting on the couch watching a TV show, and I'd start tearing up. Janine would see it and comfort me, but it wasn't only about the show we were watching – I'd changed. It was like my experience had unlocked a part of me that I'd kept buried for years.

And while the tears still come more easily now, I see it as a good thing. That vulnerability, that openness, has helped me connect with people on a deeper level, whether it's through the support groups, through advocacy work, or by simply sitting with someone in a hospital ward who feels as lost and scared as I once did.

15

FIGHTING FOR CHANGE

As I began to heal, and my fear that the cancer would come back started to ease, I was left with a burning need to make a difference. I'd made up my mind: I wanted to ban solariums.

What infuriated me the most about sunbeds was the lack of warning. Sunbed operators were supposed to provide declarations for customers to sign, acknowledging the cancer risks associated with tanning beds. But I was never asked to sign anything, not once. It was blatant negligence, and I was determined to make sure no-one else would be blindsided like I was.

At that stage, I wasn't an advocate – I was just a scared bloke trying to figure it all out – but sharing my story on *RPA* had given me a taste of how speaking up could have a positive impact, and I was keen to do more. I wanted change. But everything was new, overwhelming and frightening, and I was learning as I went. I couldn't stop wondering, *What about the people using solariums today? What about the ones tanning at the beach right now? Why didn't I know about this sooner? Why isn't anyone warning them?*

Those questions became the seed for everything that was to come. In early 2009, I reached out to the Cancer Council, desperate to channel my frustration into action, and hoping that they would be able to guide me in how to get started. A representative came out to visit me at my home in Ambarvale, and I told her my idea: to ban sunbeds across the country. She listened kindly, but it was clear she had major doubts. 'That's a big ask,' she said. 'I don't know if you'll manage it, but you can try.'

She wasn't exactly negative, but you could tell she thought I was dreaming, that the goal was too big. I didn't care. Someone had to do something, and I figured that someone might as well be me.

When she left, Janine and I just looked at each other. I said, 'Far out, this is a huge task, but we're doing it.' That's how I've always been. If I set my mind to something, I'm all in. The woman from the Cancer Council gave me a few suggestions, like doing a media course or an advocacy course, to help me get started. I had no idea what I was doing, but I was determined to figure it out.

The push to ban sunbeds was driven by a mix of personal rage and inspiration. Clare Oliver had led the fight, using the final weeks of her life to educate people about the dangers of sunbeds. She had such a massive impact in such a short time, but sunbeds still hadn't been outright banned. They were everywhere, still being used. It seemed wrong to let her efforts fade away. I didn't know Clare personally, but I felt like I owed it to her, and to myself, to pick up where she had left off.

In 2009, I connected with a remarkable woman from Victoria called Louise White. She'd lost her daughter Emily to melanoma and had thrown herself into advocacy work, channelling her grief into something powerful. It was actually Louise who encouraged Clare to speak publicly about her experience back in 2007, and she played a crucial role behind the scenes in supporting Clare's family through it all.

Louise became an incredible support for me during those early years as I learned the ropes of advocacy work, especially in the campaign to ban sunbeds. She was tireless. She also ran her own charity, the Emily Tapp Melanoma

Foundation, and every year she'd organise a walk around Melbourne to raise awareness. That's where James and I first got the idea to start the Melanoma March in Sydney. Even though Louise was carrying so much personal grief, she showed up for others, including me and my family, time and again.

I never met Clare's family in person, but I almost felt like part of their circle thanks to Louise. We were all in the same email threads and advocacy groups. Having that connection to them and other supporters of Clare's only deepened my resolve. We had a shared message: the damage sunbeds caused was not only physical but a total betrayal of trust. The harm was avoidable, and sunbed operators were failing in their duty of care. I had to do something.

I was fuelled by so many emotions: anger, fear, frustration. I couldn't stop thinking about all the people still using solariums. I'd accessed them so easily, and it terrified me that others might end up going through the same thing I was experiencing. It wasn't just about me; I wanted to protect those people, too. Plus, I didn't know how much time I had left. I was living my life three months at a time, terrified that my next scan would reveal tumours everywhere. That fear drove me harder than anything.

I signed up for the courses the woman from the Cancer Council had recommended, one on media and another on advocacy. Those three-day courses taught me how to advocate effectively, approach media outlets and write compelling press releases. One of the speakers was a former health minister, and he gave us a piece of advice that I'll never forget. He said: keep your emails short and sharp, because politicians get flooded with them. He told us that the subject line was everything – if that wasn't powerful, they wouldn't even open the email. I took that to heart. From the very earliest days of the campaign, I always made sure my emails stood out. I'd use phrases like 'Cancer Survivor on a mission' and 'Ban solariums, they caused my cancer' to grab their attention. And most of the time, it worked. I usually got responses, and rarely negative ones.

That was how it all started. I didn't have all the answers, but I had a fire inside me, and I wasn't going to let it burn out.

It's wild how quickly everything came together. What started as frustration over my own experience grew into something much larger, a mission to protect others and hold the industry accountable. It wasn't easy, but the sense of purpose it gave me was worth every ounce of effort.

•

In the beginning, it was just me and my emails. I remember emailing the Cancer Council again, taking their own advice and asking if they could partner with me. That led to a meeting at their head office in Woolloomooloo sometime in late 2009 when the campaign was starting to gain momentum. I told them I wanted to ban solariums outright. They were polite but said that, given the current situation, there was no way they could put their resources behind campaigning for a full ban. They were all for stronger regulations, but they weren't willing to spend scarce funds on a push for something they didn't feel could be realistically achieved at the time. They wished me luck and put me in touch with a few other people who might be able to help, but honestly, it felt like they weren't interested. Being such a big organisation, I guess they couldn't take a bold stand like that back then.

I was disappointed. I'd assumed they had the power and influence to help push something like this forward, but they didn't.

After the Cancer Council said they couldn't help, I got to work sending more emails. I even wrote to Alan Jones at 2GB. His response was blunt: 'The chances of you banning solariums are like closing down Bondi Beach. It's never going to happen.' That just made me even more determined. I thought, *Alright, no worries. I'll prove you wrong.*

It was tough, but I wasn't going to let up. The campaign really got going after a conversation with a mate from work, Mark. Mark was one of the few who kept in touch regularly, checking in on how I was doing. Mark suggested that his son Adrian, who was good with graphic design, might be able to help me with a website. That connection was the beginning of something big.

Adrian was a powerhouse. He not only built the website but also worked on press releases for the campaign. If I had a meeting with a politician or was planning an event, Adrian would write press releases and send them to TV stations and radio networks like 2GB and 2UE. We made a good team, figuring it out as we went along, and his technical expertise made a massive difference.

The courses I'd done gave me a bit more confidence. I would cold-call radio stations before meetings, giving them sound bites they could use on the hourly news updates. That publicity really helped get the word out. By the time I'd arrive at a rally or meeting, people would already be talking about it. It was incredible to hear: 'Sunbed campaigner and melanoma survivor Jay Allen is in Bondi today for the Sunbed Ban rally.' That exposure gave the campaign momentum, and it all came from using the skills and tricks I'd learned during those courses.

Another of the courses I'd done focused on advocacy. It taught me how to approach ministers, draft legislation and push for change. That training was a game-changer.

I learned how to write messages that made an impact, how to target the right people and how to handle all the red tape.

Another thing the advocacy course had taught me was how important it was to keep the issue on the radar. So I made a point to keep pushing, calling radio stations, pitching TV interviews and getting press releases out whenever I had a meeting scheduled. I'd get Adrian to send out a press release the night before, or in the morning. Then, on the morning of the meeting, either he or I would get on the phone, pitching the story to media outlets. Nine times out of ten, we'd manage to secure coverage, usually TV news or radio. Print was rare, but the exposure we got helped boost the campaign.

I started emailing politicians. I was trying to get support from premiers and ministers – especially health ministers – in every state. I was relentless. I wrote to politicians all over the country trying to get them to support the ban or, at the very least, have a conversation. In the beginning, most of my emails went unanswered, or were politely declined. The only real interest came from the Greens. Lee Rhiannon and John Kaye reached out, saying they liked what I was doing, and invited me to meet with them. That meeting turned out to be a turning point. Both Lee and John were incredibly supportive, not just in words but in action, too.

They didn't just tell me they liked the campaign; they helped me figure out how to make it work.

I ended up doing work experience with their team in Parliament House in Sydney for several months in late 2009 and early 2010. It was a crash course in how politics really worked. I worked in their offices, helping with press releases, watching interviews and learning the rhythm of parliamentary life. They showed me how to navigate the system, how to book meetings with the right people and how to make sure my voice and the voices of others affected were heard.

While doing that work experience, I wasn't just observing; I was taking action. I'd schedule meetings with other MPs and key stakeholders. Lee and John's support gave me credibility, as well as greater access – people were starting to listen. It was a steep learning curve, but every day, I got a better understanding of how to fight this fight. Some politicians dismissed me outright, saying a sunbed ban would never happen. I'd leave those meetings feeling defeated, but by the next morning, I'd be back at it, determined to prove them wrong.

Without Lee and John's help, I don't think the campaign would have made it off the ground the way it did. They believed in me, and they gave me the tools I needed, as well as a platform. Their support showed me that I could make a difference. Trying to change legislation felt like a massive task, but they gave me the confidence to chase that goal.

Adrian was invaluable, too. He wasn't part of a formal charity; neither of us were. We had a website, sunbedban.com, but it wasn't a registered charity or a not-for-profit. It was just the two of us, running with this idea, spurred on by our determination and a sense of urgency.

Of course, not everyone supported us. I even received a death threat once. Some guy told me he'd kill me if I kept going. That stopped me in my tracks. I thought about reporting it to the police, but in the end, I responded with my story instead. I explained why I was doing this – that it wasn't about ruining anyone's business, but about saving lives. By the end of our exchange, he said, 'Alright, I get it. I get why you're doing it.' But then he added, 'You owe me $75,000. That's what I just spent on my wife's business to install these machines. How are you going to pay it?'

I told him, 'Mate, you're going down the wrong road. I'm not giving you a cent. Do what you need to do, but I'm doing this for a reason.' After that, he backed off.

There were others, too, especially on social media. I had to block quite a few people. I used my story to defuse situations like that, never escalating a threat, email or message by responding to it with anger. I just shared what had happened to me and why I wanted to stop it happening to anyone else. Most of the time, they'd go away after hearing why I was campaigning.

At the time, solariums were everywhere – in beauticians' shops, on every street corner. I remember I'd always pass this one place with flashing lights advertising quick tans. Turned out the place was run by the same guy who'd threatened me. He turned out to be part of a biker gang, and he'd been in and out of jail. It was intimidating, but he never actually followed through on his threats. In any case, I'd faced down scarier threats in my day.

16

ON A MISSION

In 2010, I packed a bag, grabbed my mate Clint and flew to the US for what turned into a whirlwind trip across the country, from New York to Los Angeles. Clint was a melanoma survivor, too: after having thirty-five tumours throughout his body, he was now all clear. We'd become great mates, bonded by what we'd both gone through.

I'd always wanted to do a US road trip, so I floated the idea to Clint and he was on board. There just wasn't enough information here in Australia at the time about treatment or what life looked like after a diagnosis. We wanted to see what was happening in the US and connect with anyone who could help us better understand this disease and how to beat it. Together, we drew up a plan to visit treatment centres, support groups and families affected by melanoma.

It wasn't a fancy tour. We hired a car, mapped out some key stops and just went for it. It was raw, real and one of the most enlightening trips I've ever done. We spent three intense weeks crisscrossing the country, sometimes driving five or six hours at a time to visit patients, then jumping back in the car to get to the next stop. It was full-on but absolutely worth it.

What hit me straight away was how different the health-care system is over there. In Australia, we have Medicare. It's not perfect, but at least it gives us access to medical care. If you get diagnosed with skin cancer in Australia, you can at least see a specialist without having to sell your house. Over there? I was meeting people who couldn't afford even a biopsy. One young woman told me she'd waited almost a year to get a suspicious mole removed because she didn't have insurance. That floored me. A year? For something that could be deadly within months? Unbelievable.

I spoke to people who had late-stage melanoma simply because they didn't have the money to get checked sooner. It was an eye-opener. It made me realise how lucky I'd been to not only survive, but to live in a country where

I had access to the care I needed. In the US, if you don't have insurance, you're on your own. It's brutal.

We met some incredible people along the way. One couple I'll never forget was Bob and Laurie. Bob had stage 4 melanoma, and after hearing about the YouTube channel we were documenting our trip on, they invited us to stay at their place near the San Diego airport. They put us up in their guest room, took us out for lunches, cooked us dinners – just beautiful, generous people. Bob was dealing with very advanced melanoma, but seeing Clint, someone who'd survived with dozens of tumours, gave him hope. It gave *all* of us hope. Before we left, we gave Bob one of our 'Sunbed Ban' t-shirts and he wore it proudly. Bob and Laurie even documented the visit on their Facebook and YouTube channels.

Another visit that stayed with me was to Eric and his wife, Jill. Eric had over 1000 melanoma tumours in his leg. He was in constant, unimaginable pain. But the simple act of us showing up – just being there, listening, talking, sharing stories – meant everything to them. I'll never forget that.

Bob and Eric have both since passed away. But I'm still close friends with Jill and Laurie. That trip forged lifelong bonds and reminded me how powerful those connections with others can be when you're in your darkest moments.

We didn't just visit families. We were there to spread the word about melanoma, too – we gave talks, met with patient advocates, visited hospitals and just generally tried to connect with anyone who'd listen. The talks themselves were powerful. We'd speak to community groups, universities, hospitals, and we even visited the Melanoma Research Foundation in New York, which at the time was the world's leading melanoma foundation. What I found was that, despite all the cultural differences, the fear was the same. People were scared. They wanted to know how to protect themselves, and they were grateful to hear from someone who had been through it and survived. Clint and I weren't doctors, but we were living proof. And that counted for a lot.

That trip lit a fire in me again. It reminded me that this issue was global. And the more we could share our stories, the more pressure we could put on governments and institutions to take skin cancer seriously. I came home even more determined than ever to keep fighting, not just for Australians, but for anyone facing this disease without the support they deserve.

The media picked up on our trip, too. Local US news stations ran short stories, and the *Sunday Telegraph* in Australia published a piece just as we were heading off, calling it 'two Aussie survivors on a mission'. That was exactly what it was.

•

By 2011, I was more than ready to dedicate myself to the campaign full-time. We sold our house in Ambarvale and built a new one out near Tahmoor in Picton. I started volunteering for Melanoma Patients Australia (MPA), a group I connected with in Queensland, and started support groups for them alongside Herman. At last, I was able to fully commit myself to the cause – everything I did was focused on that fight.

I stayed with MPA for about two years, helping out with fundraising events and advocating for melanoma patients. But after a while, I realised that they were focused on providing support. That's incredibly important, of course, but I wanted to do more. I had this vision of setting up a mobile skin-check truck that could travel around the country, providing accessible skin checks. When I raised the idea with MPA, they weren't on board. They wanted to focus on patient support, which I totally understood. And I was still laser-focused on getting tanning beds in the bin, which wasn't their objective. That's when I started thinking about starting my own charity.

Around that time, I was frequently being asked to represent the patient voice for organisations like the Melanoma Institute Australia (MIA) and the Cancer Institute, sharing my own experience as a melanoma patient and speaking on behalf of others. Whether it was attending press conferences or sharing my story, I became a go-to spokesperson. I decided to make the most of my connections with MIA. I approached them directly and asked if they could help me start my charity.

I met with one of the leaders at MIA, at their brand-new $40 million Poche Centre in North Sydney. When I explained my idea, she said, 'Why don't you come and work here instead of starting your own charity?' The suggestion caught me off guard, but as I thought about it, I realised it made sense. The Poche Centre was a state-of-the-art facility dedicated to melanoma research and treatment. It was a massive opportunity.

An hour after I left my meeting, they called me and offered me a two-day-a-week position at MIA, starting the following week. At the same time, MPA offered me a position, three days a week with a phone included. Suddenly, after two years of being a volunteer, I had two job offers on the table, working on something I was so passionate about. It was huge. After talking it through with Janine, Herman and my mate James, I decided I'd take the MIA role. Their focus on research was key: there was no cure, and we needed one. I wanted to help, and their skin-check initiatives and the cutting-edge resources of the Poche Centre felt like the right fit.

I started at MIA in March 2011 as a community coordinator. At first, I was overwhelmed. I remember sitting at my desk, staring at the computer, thinking, *What do I even do?* I asked a member of the team for guidance, and she suggested I start contacting Rotary and Lions clubs to book speaking engagements. It was a great way to build on the public speaking I'd done in the US and to get the message out. I was nervous at first, but after all the meetings I'd had with politicians, I was starting to build confidence. I threw myself into it, speaking at clubs and events, pretty much seven days a week, working far more than the two days a week I'd been hired for.

I stayed with MIA for nearly ten years, from 2011 until December 2020. When I started, it was a small team – there were only four of us. Now, they have a staff of sixty or seventy. Looking back, I'm very proud of the role I played in helping them grow. I know I contributed to the foundation of what MIA has become today.

•

While I was working at MIA, I was also still actively campaigning to ban sunbeds. It was a slow burn at first, but I started making progress. My dad came across an article by Professor Simon Chapman AO, a leading health academic, who was also advocating for a solarium ban. I sent Simon an email, and he replied immediately, inviting me to meet with him.

I remember walking through the halls of the University of Sydney to meet him. Here I was, this truck driver from Western Sydney, stepping into this world of professors and academics. Simon's office was full of awards and ceremonial caps, and I thought, *How did I even get here?* He asked me to share my story, and I told him about my campaign. He said, 'I've heard a bit about you, and I believe in what you're doing.'

Simon was incredible. He connected me with journalists, and suggested running a poll to gauge public opinion on banning solariums. That poll showed that over eighty per cent of people supported a ban, which gave us huge momentum. News outlets picked up the story, and I ended up on shows like *Q&A* and *Hack*. Simon guided me through the media landscape, helping me seize every opportunity. It was daunting, for sure, but it just felt like something I had to do. The media or spotlight never got to me. I was on a mission to ban sunbeds, and nothing was going to get in the way.

Between Simon's support and my persistence, things started to take off. I spoke at forums, went on radio programs and even attended high-profile events like Chris O'Brien Lifehouse dinners. For those who don't know the name, the late Professor Chris O'Brien AO was a respected Australian surgeon who dedicated his life to treating cancer. As it happens, he was actually known to many people from his appearances on the *RPA* TV show. After being diagnosed with brain cancer himself in 2006, Chris became a passionate advocate for integrated cancer care. His dream was an all-in-one cancer centre – Lifehouse – where patients could get all aspects of their cancer treatment under the one roof, from diagnosis and surgery to chemo and therapy. At the time, there was nothing like it in Australia. Sadly, Chris passed away in 2009 before the centre was finished, but his legacy lives on through Lifehouse. It's an incredible centre that helps tens of thousands of Australians going through cancer every year. To have a seat at the table at those Lifehouse events was a huge foot in the door for me and my cause.

Every step of the way, I pushed for change, and slowly, it started to happen.

Media became a key part of the campaign. I was starting to attract some media attention, and I even managed to get segments on *A Current Affair*, where I talked about the campaign to ban solariums. I also went on *Sunrise* and *The Today Show* a few times. There was one memorable *Sunrise* interview where I had two whole chickens from Woolies I'd brought with me to use as props. The plan was to hold them up live on air to illustrate the point I was making, but I got so nervous that I completely forgot about them! I was kicking myself afterward.

I made up for it, though, at a community cabinet meeting in mid-2011. Barry O'Farrell, Premier of New South Wales at the time, was there, along with the entire cabinet. I held up a raw chicken and said, 'This is someone freshly out of school; this is their skin before they start tanning.' Then I held up a burnt, blackened chicken, oil dripping down my arm, and said, 'This is what your skin looks like after using solariums or tanning excessively. The cells are damaged beyond repair. This is what you don't see happening underneath.'

It grabbed everyone's attention. The next day, there was a photo of me with the chickens in the *Daily Telegraph*. That moment was even voted one of the most memorable photos of the year by one of the local papers, the *Macarthur Advertiser*. They used to run articles about me almost monthly, and it was a huge boost, getting everyone talking and sharing about the campaign on social media.

The idea of using props and sharing stories came from a combination of the Cancer Council advocacy course and people like Simon Chapman and Juliette O'Brien, Chris O'Brien's daughter. Simon was incredibly strategic, always encouraging me to aim high. Juliette, who worked at Triple J, also gave me invaluable advice. One thing she shared, something her dad used to say, was to remember that in live interviews, you've got limited time, so it's important to make sure you get your key points across, no matter what.

Every time I spoke, I'd make sure to mention the campaign, the data and the support we needed from politicians. I'd also weave in personal stories to drive home the human impact of the issue. These stories were powerful; they connected people to the cause and made it impossible to ignore. That approach, along with the media training I'd had and Simon's guidance, helped me secure a huge amount of coverage. It wasn't easy, but I knew I had to keep the issue on everyone's radar.

I was driven. I knew I had one opportunity with these live interviews. One time, when I managed to get a spot on *Q&A*, I had just thirty seconds. I'd have my notes in front of me, dot points, and I'd just go for it. Every interview,

I'd try to keep the conversation going, always finding a way to keep the focus on the campaign.

Over time, I got better at getting my point across, especially with live interviews. I learned to use that final question the journalist asks to squeeze in one last message. When they'd say, 'Thanks for coming in,' I'd respond, 'No worries. And if you'd like more information, go to my website,' or something similar. I always made sure to get that in.

I always dressed well for interviews, too. Presentation mattered. My sister Chantal worked in a few great men's fashion stores, so I'd often rope her in for advice on what to wear. She had an eye for what looked sharp, and I knew that looking put-together gave the campaign a sense of credibility.

One day, I was in Melbourne for a melanoma awareness lunch, walking past Parliament House with a few mates, including my good friend Paul White, another melanoma survivor. We spotted the then Victorian health minister, David Davis, mid-press conference on the steps. I'd written to him countless times before, with no reply. Paul turned to me and said, 'Go on, Jay. Do your thing.'

So I did.

I calmly walked up and introduced myself. 'Hi Mr Davis, I'm Jay Allen. I'm running a campaign to ban solariums.

I've written to you many times but haven't had a response.' He looked stunned – completely caught off guard – but he nodded, thanked me and returned to the press conference.

I don't know if it made the news that day, but I noticed a few cameras swing my way. A couple of weeks later, I received a letter from his office. Not long after that, I was invited in for a meeting. During that conversation, he acknowledged that banning solariums was something they were seriously considering. It was a small moment, but it proved again that showing up and speaking up could make things happen.

The first real sign that change was on the horizon came from New South Wales. Simon organised a meeting with Frank Sartor, who was the Minister Assisting the Minister for Health (Cancer) at the time, and we went in with the Cancer Institute. I'll never forget it. Frank was sitting there, and the meeting wasn't going great. We were losing him. I needed to shock him into the realisation that action was the only option here. So I said, 'For those under thirty-five, there's up to a seventy-five per cent higher risk of getting melanoma.' And straight away, Frank said, 'Let's ban them for under-25s and under-35s. Let's see what we can do.'

After that meeting, he announced new measures. They were going to legislate that people under twenty-five could only use solariums once every three months, and under-35s only once every two months. It was a step in the right direction, but unfortunately, Frank didn't get re-elected, and the legislation was scrapped. That was disappointing, but we kept going.

Claire Harvey from the *Sunday Telegraph* was a huge help. When Frank wasn't re-elected, Claire did a feature about it, calling me the 'disappointed solarium campaigner'. That exposure kept the story alive. Early on, I was told to nurture relationships with journalists and value the exposure I got. I never took it for granted, and I would thank them for articles they'd written and offer to stay in touch. I did that every time. Some of those journalists are now chiefs of staff at major networks. I call them if I need help, and they always do their best.

When Jillian Skinner became the Minister for Health in 2011, we had to start from scratch with her government. I met with her, and also reached out to Tony Abbott's office and Julia Gillard's office. I remember sitting with a member of Tony Abbott's staff in Sydney. He said, 'Keep going. I've spoken to Tony, and he says to keep doing what you can.' That encouragement kept me pushing forward. Social media helped keep the momentum alive, too. It was all about staying consistent and keeping the message out there, and at the front of people's minds.

Jillian Skinner was incredibly supportive when she came on board. She told me outright, 'Look, they should be banned, and I'll do everything I can to help you.' I was in regular contact with her office, sending emails back and forth and attending meetings. I even bumped into her once at an event for Chris O'Brien Lifehouse at Government House Sydney, and she told me to keep going, saying that she'd back me. Her office, along with Simon, suggested starting a petition, so we did, both online and on paper. We'd go out to places like Bondi Beach, set up a marquee, wear campaign t-shirts and ask people to sign the petition. It was full-on, but it really helped gather momentum.

All of this was self-funded. I didn't get any grants or financial support from anyone – it was just me. Herman was often there beside me, too – he was always supportive of everything I did. At the time, I was still working two days a week at MIA, which gave me the flexibility to spend the rest of my time on the campaign.

•

Through all of this, life kept moving for Janine and me. Our family kept growing. After Jaxon's birth in November 2008, which brought so much joy into our lives just as we were beginning to find our feet again, along came Charli, our beautiful daughter, in August 2011. Her arrival added even more love and noise to our home. Around that time, Janine, who had been doing nails as a beautician, gave that up because of concerns about the UV exposure. After seeing what I'd gone through, she was worried about what it meant for her own health – and it didn't sit right with the campaign's message, either – so she decided to focus on being a full-time mum instead. It was the latest in a long line of selfless actions that allowed us to make this mission possible.

Several years later, in October 2018, Janine and I welcomed another daughter, Chloe. Her timing felt like a new chapter, a reminder of how far we'd come. And then, just when we thought we had our hands full, Josie arrived in December 2020, rounding out our little pack. Each of my kids came into my world during very different chapters of my life, but every one of them brought a renewed sense of purpose, joy and healing. They've kept me grounded, kept me laughing and reminded me what all the fighting was for.

17

THE MELANOMA MAN

By 2012, things were really moving. I remember exactly where I was when I found out that we'd won: the ban was going through. I was driving down to Wollongong, organising a golf day for MIA. I was handing out proposals to sponsors when I got a call from the Environment Department, the decision-makers behind a potential ban. It was such an emotional moment. I still remember the exact stretch of road I was on. I saw the number flash up and pulled over. When I heard the words, 'They're banning them, Jay. It's going through,' I just broke. I didn't even try to hold it in. I sat in the car, hands shaking, head against the steering wheel, sobbing.

All those years of fighting, of knocking on doors, sending email after email, of activism from Clare Oliver, of politicians telling me it would never happen – they had finally paid off. They were banning solariums in New South Wales. No longer would people walk into one of those rooms thinking it was harmless, only to end up like I did, all scarred, terrified and wondering if they'd ever see their kids grow up.

They explained that the legislation would be announced soon, accompanied by a big media rollout. The ban would come into effect at the end of 2014 to give businesses time to adapt to the legislated changes and remove their sunbeds. But from then on, sunbeds would be outlawed throughout the state. 'Well done,' they said. 'You've played a big part in this. But you need to keep it quiet for now. Don't say a word to anyone.'

I was speechless.

I couldn't help but think: what if this had happened earlier? What if solariums had been banned before I ever set foot in one? Would I have avoided cancer altogether? Would I have spared my family that pain, been able to avoid the surgeries, the scans, the sleepless nights worrying that I was going to die? I'll never know. But what I do know is that because of that ban, loads of other people get to avoid it all. I can live with that.

It was as if a huge load had lifted off my shoulders. Like the years of fear and grief and guilt had actually been for something – I had something to show for everything I'd been through. I didn't just survive; I did something with the pain I'd experienced. I turned it into change. And in that moment, sitting in my car, wiping tears off my face, I felt so proud. Properly proud. Not just for me, but for everyone who stood beside me. Together, we had done this enormous thing. We had actually saved lives.

After the call, I rang my wife and then Simon to let them know. I couldn't share the news with anyone else, as it was still confidential, but that didn't take away from the moment. Even now, whenever I drive down that same road to Wollongong, I think about that call and how it felt. It's something I'll never forget.

The Cancer Council wanted to host the press conference for the announcement at their head office in Woolloomooloo. I was a bit frustrated by that, given that I'd done all the heavy lifting. In the end, the press conference was held at the MIA office, at the Poche Centre in North Sydney, where I was working at the time. That moment was about the people who had truly fought for the ban for many years. We'd worked bloody hard for that moment.

Once the ban was announced in New South Wales, I knew it would create a domino effect. I'd learned that, typically, when one state implements something like this, others follow. And so I doubled down on campaigning. I started taking red-eye flights to places like Perth and Victoria, meeting with health ministers and other officials. Those quiet one-on-one discussions really made a difference.

In Queensland, two sisters who'd lost their mum to melanoma joined the campaign. In Victoria, I had help from Professor Grant McArthur AO, a leading cancer oncologist who was instrumental in the Victorian sunbed ban. He'd sometimes call me and say, 'Jay, we're holding a press conference on solariums tomorrow. Can you make it?' I'd book a flight that night or early the next morning to make sure I was there. I never wanted to miss an opportunity, and I wasn't afraid to hustle.

Around that time, cancer epidemiologist and good friend of mine Professor Anne Cust released a research paper confirming that solariums caused cancer. The World Health Organization also declared solariums carcinogenic. These developments added weight to the campaign.

I even circled back to Alan Jones, who'd told me banning solariums was impossible. I wrote to him, sharing the news of the ban, and reminded him of what he'd said. He wrote back, congratulating me. From there, he began inviting me onto his radio show whenever I had events or updates to share. Similarly, Ray Hadley and others at 2GB became strong supporters, frequently giving me airtime to talk about what I was doing.

Once New South Wales made the decision, the other states got on board pretty quickly. I remember being on a family holiday in a campervan, and I had to stop by the side of the road to do a live cross for a TV interview. They wanted to talk about the upcoming solarium ban in South Australia. No matter where I was, I made sure I showed up for these opportunities.

•

Around this time, people started calling me 'The Melanoma Man'. People affected by melanoma would recognise me and say, 'Oh, you're the melanoma guy!' It started to catch on. A mate of mine suggested I embrace it, but I wasn't entirely comfortable with it at first. I didn't want to be defined by melanoma. But over time, I've come to see it as part of the mission.

It took me a couple of years to get used to the name, but in 2015, I started a Facebook page called 'The Melanoma Man'. That page now has over 50,000 followers, and it's become an incredible source of support, not just for me, but for others dealing with melanoma. When I put up stories of people going through treatment, the amount of support that pours in from around the world is incredible. It's become a real community.

It's funny – I don't document everything, but there's a lot on that old Facebook page. I've left it up partly for my family, so one day they can look back and see what I was doing all those years. I've left up the 'Sunbedban' Facebook page, too. I'm happy that those memories will still be there in years to come, for my kids to see how mad their dad was (just kidding).

Although my focus was Australia, I always kept an eye on what was going on around the world. During the campaign to ban sunbeds, Brazil was a big point of reference for me. They were the first country in the world to ban solariums, so I always used them as an example. I'd say, 'Brazil has done it, why can't Australia?' I even did a few Skype interviews with media agencies in Brazil.

Later on, I started working with Melanoma UK. I went over there in 2018 and helped launch a campaign in Manchester. I did some advocacy work and met with key politicians, including some in the British health system. It got a bit of media attention and sparked some conversation, but banning solariums in the UK is a tough battle. The industry is massive, and the government makes so much money from it. Honestly, I don't think it'll ever happen. Then again, that's what people used to tell me about Australia.

It's the same in the US. I went over there to try and push the campaign, but it's a completely different ball game. It's such a powerful industry, and frankly, I didn't want to stir things up too much, didn't want to risk getting myself into trouble.

When the ban finally came through on 31 December 2014 in New South Wales, I didn't really take time to celebrate. People would say, 'Oh, you're amazing!' But I didn't feel that way. I wasn't in it for recognition. I was just happy to be alive and focused on saving lives. But there were some acknowledgements along the way, which was nice. In 2014, I was named one of the 25 Most Influential People in the Not-for-Profit Sector. It was nice to see the campaign being recognised in that way.

I was also lucky enough to be nominated for the Pride of Australia Medal in 2018. I made it to the finals for that one but just missed out. The big one for me was being named a finalist in the Australian of the Year Awards in the Local Hero category in 2017. That was such a proud moment. But honestly, my biggest achievement to date was being awarded the Order of Australia Medal (OAM) in 2021. That recognition really hit home. It felt like a culmination of everything I'd worked for over the years. I dedicated that medal to all those affected by melanoma, and to all the mates I'd lost.

The sunbed ban was the moment everything started. It's still one of my greatest achievements: getting New South Wales over the line at the end of 2014, and then seeing the rest of the country follow by 2016. Those were monumental years, and I'll always look back on them with pride.

•

As the sunbed bans started rolling out across the country, I was still busy with MIA. The momentum from the campaign carried over into other areas of my work. But things at MIA had started to change. The organisation had grown, and as often happens when organisations get large, things became more bureaucratic. It didn't feel like quite the right fit for me anymore.

I have no doubt that taking that job at MIA set me on the path to where I am today. They gave me the foundation and training I needed, and it was an incredible opportunity for me to learn and grow. But as the organisation grew larger, every decision I made had to go through multiple layers of approval. New managers were coming in, each with their own ideas, and I felt like my ideas weren't cutting through. My confidence took a hit, and I knew I needed to make a change.

Around this time, a friend of mine said to me, 'Jay, you've got the platform, the passion and the experience. Why not start your own charity?' I realised he was right – I'd already given it a lot of thought, and it was the perfect time to do this. I could start fresh and focus on what I felt was most important.

So in 2020, just before the pandemic, I made the decision to leave MIA and start my own charity. It wasn't an easy choice, but looking back, it was the right one. Leaving a salaried job was risky, but sometimes, you just know it's time to take a different path.

There were so many highlights from my time at MIA, but the walks I did to raise awareness and funds for melanoma research will always hold a special place in my heart. They were physically demanding, but also deeply emotional journeys.

It all started in 2014 with the first walk from Sydney to Melbourne, which was 900 kilometres on foot – just me and another melanoma survivor, Andrew. It was isolating at times, but we had four support vehicles provided by Toyota, all decked out in campaign branding, and we still managed to raise $250,000. That walk taught me a lot about resilience and about how many people were willing to rally behind the cause.

By 2017, I wanted the walk to be about more than just fundraising. I wanted to give people the opportunity to walk for someone they'd lost or were supporting through melanoma. We had people join us each day, each with their own story and fundraising page, and together we raised close to $300,000. We powered through torrential rain in Coffs Harbour, swapping out our socks and shoes every thirty minutes, but the shared purpose pushed us forward. We crossed the finish line at Barangaroo in Sydney, greeted by hundreds of supporters. It was overwhelming in the best possible way.

Then came 2019. The big one. I walked 2000 kilometres from Adelaide to Sydney in just fifty days. It was brutal. I had blisters on blisters by the end of it. One day, coming out of Victoria, I popped fifteen blisters with a hot needle! But I never once got in a support car. I walked every single kilometre, because how could I not? I was walking beside people who had lost loved ones to melanoma or were fighting it themselves. When your feet hurt, you'd just look next to you and see someone who'd lost their mum, their kid, their best mate, and you'd keep going.

That walk raised an incredible $750,000, helping to fund a brain trial for melanoma patients. Over 300 people joined me on that journey, and it was a team effort in every way. Toyota vehicles, clothing sponsors, Woolies and Coles lunch vouchers, and a road crew who managed food, drinks, logistics, and even tended to our sore feet, all helped along the way.

Every event took twelve months of planning, but it was all worth it. We couldn't have done any of it without the amazing volunteers who showed up again and again. James has helped me plan every walk. He's been a rock.

I trained hard for the walks, too. A year out, I'd be doing ten kilometres morning and night, with forty-kilometre training walks from Maroubra to Watsons Bay and back on the weekends. I even met Pat Farmer, the ultra-marathon legend, who told me the secret was fifty per cent passion, fifty per cent preparation. That advice stuck with me, especially after one volunteer doubted I'd finish the 2017 walk – he thought it was just too much for one person to do. I used that as fuel. I was never going to quit, not when patients can't take a break from their treatment and families can't take a break from the grief of losing their loved ones.

The walks did take a toll on my body – mostly weight loss and those nasty blisters – but the training turned me into a machine. And every step felt like it meant something. Sadly, many of the amazing people who walked with me – patients, volunteers, mates – have since passed away. But their memory is stitched into every walk and every dollar raised. I carry them with me in everything I do.

Best of all, Janine and the kids were there for each one. They'd always find a way to surprise me mid-walk, running up with huge smiles.

•

I was also running support groups for MIA from 2011 right through to when I left in 2020. Those groups meant a lot to me. Being able to give patients hope and show them they weren't alone was an amazing privilege. Of course, there were heartbreaking moments, too. I've lost so many friends over the years, people I connected with through these walks and groups. But knowing I could make a difference in their lives, even if only for a short while, made it all worthwhile.

During that time, I also had access to some of the smartest minds in the world when it came to melanoma. I used to rope them into coming to our support group meetings as guest speakers – legends like Professor Richard Scolyer AO, one of the world's leading melanoma pathologists, and Associate Professor Jonathan Stretch, a brilliant surgeon. These guys were on another level. I've always had so much respect for them, not just for their brains but for their hearts. They supported me beyond the clinic, sending messages during the big walks, even joining us on the road when they could to check in and keep me going. And then there's Professor John Thompson AO, the absolute king of melanoma globally and one of the original pioneers of melanoma treatment. Just being around these guys made me feel like we were really making progress.

Leaving MIA was bittersweet. I was ready for a change. I found myself at the start of a new decade, about to start a new charity, while trying to wrap my head around the highs and lows of the past one. But that's life, isn't it? You just keep moving forward. One step at a time.

Gradually, I started to feel like myself again. I was clear-headed, healthy, and I was gearing up to focus on my own charity.

But then, in late 2020, the lump on my neck appeared.

18

ROUND TWO

It was small at first, but when I shaved, I could feel it under my skin.

I told myself it was probably nothing, but deep down, I knew something was wrong. The lump was hard, like a rock, and there was no pain, which I knew wasn't a good sign. When I finally got it checked at the start of 2021, two ultrasounds didn't show anything, so I was told I needed to get a fine needle biopsy. The biopsy confirmed it: I had squamous cell carcinoma. Skin cancer. Again.

Hearing the word 'cancer' for the second time was devastating. All I could think was, *Not again.* My mind went into overdrive, imagining the worst-case scenario. Had it spread? Was it too late? Had my luck run out? The weekend before the results came back, my anxiety was through the roof. I remember pacing around the kitchen table, my hands on my head. I was shaking. Janine kept telling me to calm down, but it's hard to explain the sheer terror that takes over when you're waiting for results like that. At the time, I thought it was melanoma again, and I knew all too well the battle I was in for if it was.

The shock on my family's faces when I told them said it all. But as they've always done, they rallied around me. No hesitation. Just love and support.

My mum was calm in that stoic way only she can be. 'You'll be right, son,' she told me. 'I've got a good feeling you'll be okay.' I clung to those words more than I let on. Janine was the same, reassuring me and keeping me grounded. 'We got through it once,' she said. 'We'll get through it again.' Even though this round of treatment was the toughest thing I've ever endured, I never doubted I could make it through with them in my corner.

The kids responded in their own way. Jaxon and Charli understood everything. They'd grown up in the charity space with me, meeting so many people over the years who were battling melanoma, so many of whom are no longer with us. I think it's given them a rare kind of compassion. They're better humans for it. We've always tried to shield them from the hardest parts, but they've seen enough to understand what it means to fight for something bigger than yourself.

My youngest girls, Chloe and Josie, still don't know the full extent of what I've been through. They know what I do and they get a kick out of seeing me on TV sometimes, but beyond that, cancer is a bit of an abstract concept to them. Maybe I'll tell them one day.

After the diagnosis, the doctor ordered a scan to confirm if there had been any spread. When the results finally came in, I got a mix of good and bad news. The cancer was localised, just in my neck and throat, but it was still serious. I started treatment in February 2021. It was chemo and head and neck radiation, five days a week for seven weeks. I'd been through tough times before, but nothing could have prepared me for how brutal that treatment would be.

I'd listen to the *Rocky* soundtrack during every radiation session. The sessions themselves only lasted five or six minutes, but they were brutal. Still, I pushed through, because I knew what was at stake.

The radiation targeted my head and neck, and it felt like my body was being destroyed from the inside out. The blisters in my throat made eating unbearable. Imagine the worst sunburn you've ever had, but inside your throat. I'd gargle with Xylocaine to numb the pain long enough to force down a few bites of food, but even that soon became impossible. The chemo stripped me of any appetite, and the weight started falling off. I lost fourteen kilos during those seven weeks. By the end of March, around my birthday, they had to admit me to the hospital. I lived on ice blocks, morphine and Panadol. The pain medication wore off every four hours, so I would wake up throughout the night in agony. I don't have words for how bad the pain was. I was completely drained – physically, emotionally, in every way possible.

Janine was my rock, as always. Josie was only a baby when I started treatment, just two months old, so Janine already had so much on her plate, but she held me together and looked after the whole family by herself with her usual incredible strength. She'd pack all the kids into the car to run to the chemist for supplies or make late-night trips to get ice for my throat. I wouldn't have made it through without her.

It's funny – when I was first diagnosed with melanoma over a decade ago, I didn't know anything about cancer. I was terrified, because I didn't understand what was happening. This time, I knew too much. I knew all the statistics, and so many stories of people who didn't make it, and all of that was running through my head. That knowledge gave me the tools to cope, but it also made me hyper-aware of everything that could go wrong.

Through it all, the Cancer Council and Can Assist were a godsend. They'd send cars to pick me up for treatment when I was too weak to drive, send me vouchers to make things easier and organise calls of support. Those little acts of kindness meant the world, honestly.

So many people rallied around me during that time. It was heartwarming to see how many people stepped up, bringing food to the house or just checking in. It felt like all the support I'd given over the past ten or so years had come full circle. People I'd helped before were now showing up for me, and it gave me so much strength.

One woman who really stepped up during my treatment was Jane Mahony. She was a nurse, a melanoma survivor herself and a bloody good human. Jane would drive me all the way from the Southern Highlands to Sydney for my appointments. It was a six-hour round trip for her. At first, we'd talk the whole way there and back, sharing stories. But as the treatment wore me down, I'd often just sleep the whole drive. Jane never complained. She just showed up, quietly doing what needed to be done. She helped me enormously, especially with the pain in my throat, which got pretty intense toward the end.

Most of the people who supported me during that time had been touched by melanoma in some way. That created an immediate bond between us. James, as always, was there as well, as was my mate Anthony 'Simmo' Simmons, who was going through melanoma himself, yet still found time to drive me to appointments and call me every day to check in. That's just the kind of bloke he was.

Losing Simmo about a year later was devastating. It still hurts. We'd had so many deep conversations on those drives about life, about our families, about what really matters. He went through hell – including a massive operation to remove a tumour, which actually worked – but it was an infection that got him in the end. His death was sudden, and it gutted me. But through it all, Simmo taught me a lot about strength and about showing up for people no matter what you're facing yourself. He was a legend of a human, and I'll carry his memory with me always.

Even now, I don't know how I made it through those months. But I did, and I came out the other side even more determined to make a difference. That's still what keeps me going, the idea that maybe, just maybe, my story can help someone else.

One woman who brought meals told me later, 'We honestly didn't think you were going to make it. You looked so sick.'

At the time, I didn't see it that way. I just thought, *I'm in hospital, I'll get better.* But looking back, I can see why people were worried. I'd lost so much weight, my clothes didn't fit. Some days, I'd forget to eat altogether. I had no appetite. The treatment was absolutely brutal. People see you looking frail and assume the worst, but it wasn't the cancer that was killing me; it was the treatment – it took such a toll.

One morning, the doctors let me out for thirty minutes to do a live cross with James Tobin from Channel 7, right outside St Vincent's Hospital. A few weeks earlier, I had launched a fundraising page for Tour de Cure to support their amazing cancer research, and this segment was to help raise funds and awareness. We ended up raising around $20,000, which was an incredible effort by so many of our supporters.

I was really unwell at the time. I'd lost a lot of weight and was often very weak. After the segment aired, I received a flood of messages and phone calls from people who had seen me and were genuinely worried. I remember going to a cafe nearby with the crew afterward to grab a green tea, but I was so sick I could barely manage a few sips. My throat felt like it was on fire. I couldn't eat or drink much at all by that stage, and the goal was to somehow get 2500 calories into me each day. I was struggling.

Later that day, I got a call from Dennis Wilson, the husband of the Governor of New South Wales, Margaret Beazley. I knew Dennis from our charity walks that finished at Government House. He asked, 'Jay, we're worried about you. Can we come and visit?' I said, 'Of course.' A few days later, they came to see me in hospital. Looking back now, it feels pretty surreal. The hospital had been told about their visit and moved me to the executive wing, a bigger room with an ensuite and a small lounge. It was a lovely gesture and a really special moment during such a tough time. I was so sick but their kindness meant so much to me. They didn't have to visit, but they did. It just shows the kind of people they are.

It worked, though. The treatment cured the cancer, but not without leaving scars. They'd warned me it was one of the most brutal treatments you could go through, and they weren't kidding. There were moments when the doctors thought I might not make it. I'd sit there in the hospital, too weak to move, wondering how much more my body could take. But somewhere mixed in with all that pain, there was still hope. I clung to the idea that this was temporary, that I'd get through it.

Even now, there's always that little bit of fear that something might come back. I had a scan this year, and they found a tiny lesion behind my nose. I was nervous at first, but they reassured me it was likely benign. Years ago, I would have panicked, demanded more scans. But now, I trust the experts. And I trust myself to not lean into the anxiety.

19

A NEW CHAPTER

In December 2021, we officially launched the Australian Skin Cancer Foundation at Bondi Beach. We had started work on building the foundation at the start of the year and were planning an earlier launch, but after I was diagnosed in February, everything was put on hold. Once my treatment finished in May and I was starting to feel better, it was full steam ahead.

The launch wasn't flashy – just a marquee, some banners and a thousand ideas – but it felt like turning a new page. A fresh start after everything I'd been through.

Setting up a charity isn't easy, but it's not impossible, either. You just take it step by step. You just need a good team around you, and I was incredibly lucky to have a solid network of people who believed in me. My friend Eve Brown, who's now our chairman, was one of my biggest supporters. Eve is an ex-lawyer, and she knew the ins and outs of setting up a charity.

With Eve's guidance and the help of others in my corner, we built something meaningful. The charity's mission is simple: we advocate, educate, fund research and, most importantly, support those battling melanoma. It's all about helping people.

I'm very proud that the foundation punches way above its weight when it comes to fundraising. One of our most meaningful contributions has come through the Mission Melanoma walks. After our very first walk, we were able to invest $100,000 into the BETTER clinical trial, which targets melanoma brain metastases. That trial is now expanding thanks to community support, with our charity donating another $110,000 to bring in more patients, hospitals and international collaborators.

Another campaign close to my heart was the 633-kilometre walk from Merimbula to Melbourne, through which we raised $100,000 for a clinical trial at Chris O'Brien Lifehouse. That trial is focused on immunotherapy for squamous cell carcinoma, aiming to reduce the need for invasive surgery in patients.

We also contributed $30,000 toward research at MIA during the 2024 Melanoma March in Dubbo, which was raised by my 333-kilometre Canberra-to-Sydney walk.

It's amazing to see how far we've come. The momentum keeps building, and I really feel that we're making a difference. It's not about the size of the events or the number of followers; it's about the lives we're touching. Every day, I'm reminded why this work matters so much.

Having lived through cancer myself, the support side of what we do at the charity means so much to me. I know what a massive difference it can make. When you hear the word 'melanoma', your brain goes to the physical stuff first: moles that change, surgery, scars. Or the brutal treatment – chemo, immunotherapy, radiation, not to mention the side effects. Fatigue that knocks you about. Nausea that won't go away. Your body stops feeling like your own.

But the mental side? That's just as tough. The fear. The anxiety. The waiting. Wondering if it's going to come back. Wondering how long you've got. And it's not just you – it's your partner, your kids, your mates. They ride every bump with you.

Financially, it's rough, too. Even with Medicare and public hospitals, there are gaps. Travel costs, time off work, private scans, ongoing monitoring – it all adds up.

Melanoma doesn't just hit individuals. It hits families and communities. And at the foundation, we'll keep fighting to make sure no-one has to face skin cancer alone or uninformed. We do everything we can to push for awareness and early detection, and to help patients get the care they need, no matter where they live.

More than ten years on from the solarium ban coming into effect, it's incredible to think about the ripple effects it's had. I'd like to think that by stopping people from using solariums, we've prevented a huge amount of harm. Prior to the ban, people were walking into solariums that delivered UV radiation six times the strength of summer midday sun. Knowing that's not possible anymore feels amazing. I'm so proud.

That said, skin cancer rates have actually gone up. That might sound bad, but I think it's because there's greater awareness these days. More people are getting their skin checked now, which is fantastic. Some dermatologists are booked out a year in advance, and clinics are at capacity. The challenge now is making those checks accessible and affordable, which is part of why we've introduced the Skin Check Truck.

The Skin Check Truck is one of the projects I'm most proud of. It's Australia's first mobile national clinic dedicated to skin cancer detection, offering free full-body skin checks and education on skin cancer prevention. The truck travels all over Australia, from regional centres to remote communities, as well as to public events, workplaces and schools, bringing expert services to people who might not otherwise have access to them. Our goal is to make skin checks available for everyone in the country, no matter where they live.

Our truck team examines people's skin, takes dermoscopic images of anything that looks suspicious and refers them for follow-ups with local doctors or dermatologists. So far, the truck has completed nearly 12,000 skin checks across 150 communities. In the process, we've detected more than 5000 non-melanoma skin cancers and 166 melanomas.

Finding the truck itself was down to an incredible man called Jason Laurie. Jason had lost his sister-in-law to melanoma, and his wife, Renee, reached out to me after hearing I was looking for a mobile clinic. She said, 'Can I pass your number on to my husband?' and once I said yes, everything fell into place. Jason found an old BreastScreen truck sitting in Macksville in New South Wales and within twenty-four hours, I was on the road heading up there while Jason drove down from the Gold Coast to meet me.

When I saw it, this big white truck, I knew straight away it was perfect. We managed to get it for a great price and got to work transforming it. It was already fitted out with awnings, clinical rooms, a kitchen and a small reception area, but we fitted new walls and new seating, wrapped it in our branding and gave it a name that said it all: *Australia's Skin Check Truck.*

Since then, Jason and I have spoken weekly, coordinating operations and mapping out where the truck will go next. Jason never chases credit or recognition; he just wants to make a difference. I like to think that, together, that's what we're doing.

The charity, though, has its own hurdles. Every dollar in and out matters, and the responsibility never really switches off for me. But I'm lucky to have smart, trustworthy people around me who help keep everything moving forward and on track.

Our biggest donors are often the people who've been directly supported by us and those who know firsthand what it means to be seen and helped during one of the hardest times in their lives. They're the ones truly invested in our mission. Their support keeps the charity going and our Skin Check Truck on the road, saving lives.

Despite how tiring it can be, I've always believed that if you're doing something for the right reasons, it'll work out.

And we're careful not to overextend ourselves financially. To keep costs down, we rely a lot on volunteers, many of whom have personal connections to melanoma. Some are students doing communications degrees, and they're fantastic. They've lost someone to melanoma and want to give back, which makes their contributions even more meaningful.

Running my own charity is definitely a 24/7 commitment. Even when I try to take a day off, I end up doing work – that's just how it is. But I've learned to listen to my team. If they tell me to step back or rethink something, I take that feedback seriously. It's a team effort, and I rely on them as much as they rely on me.

At the end of the day, this work isn't about me – it's about the team. It's about collaboration, integrity and making a genuine difference in people's lives. That's the core of what we do, and it's what keeps me going every day.

•

The charity was built on the work I've done since my first diagnosis, and wouldn't be possible without the many people who influenced and changed me along the way. Melinda Beaumont's story, for example, has always stuck with me. In 2016, she was diagnosed with stage 3 melanoma, and we became close friends. Tragically, the disease came back, and it was devastating to watch her go through it. I remember sitting with her and asking, 'Is there anything you'd really like to do?' I've always tried to do little things like that for patients, giving them meaningful experiences while they can still enjoy them. She told me she'd always wanted to take her family to the Canberra Zoo, where you can stay overnight and have the animals roam around your accommodation.

I reached out to the zoo and managed to secure a family ticket for her, but when I called her to share the news, she was in hospital, and she was too unwell to go. She was in tears, and it broke my heart. Little moments like that, where you just want to give someone a bit of happiness in such a hard time, stay with you.

Melinda passed away at Christmas in 2018, but her memory lives on in everything we do. Her family still helps me with the charity. Melinda's husband, Dean, is incredibly smart and supportive. He helps me day-to-day, and his daughter, Summah, has jumped in to help with PR. Their support reminds me why I do what I do. It's all about the people we've touched and the lives we've changed.

There was also Nicole Gillespie, who told me her dream was to go on the field during State of Origin and hold the shield for Queensland if they won. I reached out to the Queensland Origin manager, and we made it happen. In

2014, at the stadium in Sydney, Nicole got to hold up the shield when Queensland won the series. Moments like that are so special. Nicole's family has stayed connected with me, too, and that means a lot.

Whether it's helping someone get to the Logies or fulfilling other personal wishes, I've always tried to go above and beyond. And those connections don't end; they circle back, and the people I've helped often become part of the charity in some way. It's really humbling.

Looking ahead, I'd love to see the charity expand even further, particularly our mobile Skin Check Trucks. As this book goes to print, we are gearing up to launch our second Skin Check Truck. It will have its own biopsy room and a world-first mobile VECTRA WB360 machine for 3D full-body scanning, too. It will be a one-stop shop for skin checks for all Australians, but particularly for those in rural communities who otherwise might not have access to those services.

We've had plenty of meetings with politicians, but we don't receive government funding for our Skin Check Trucks yet. I know it will happen one day; we just need to keep doing what we're doing.

I'm so proud to work alongside our amazing volunteers and our truck teams out on the road. Sometimes people see me behind the wheel and say, 'You're the CEO – shouldn't other people be doing this?' But for me, it's important to be out there in the community, connecting with people and making sure that every single person who comes into our truck has a good experience and follows up on their referral, if they come away with one. If one day we have trucks rolled out across the country and every Australian has access to a free skin check, then maybe I'll sit back and say, 'Job done.' But we're not there yet.

The thing that sets the Australian Skin Cancer Foundation apart is that our volunteers are people who've been personally affected by melanoma. They get it. It's more than a job for them; it's a passion. That connection makes such a difference in how we work and what we can achieve.

The charity keeps me going, and I'm surrounded by an incredible team. It's funny to think how far we've come since launching. Sometimes it feels like we've been around forever, but it's still so new. And there's still so much work to do.

20
BRIGHTER DAYS AHEAD

I feel like I'm in a good place now, physically and mentally. These days, when I look in the mirror, I see more than the man who battled melanoma, I see the person who's come through it. I still have regular check-ups and scans, and my world still tilts a little each time I get the all clear, but each check is a reminder: treatment saved me, and catching it early was the thing that mattered most.

Melanoma remains one of Australia's most significant health challenges. It's diagnosed more frequently in Australia than almost anywhere else in the world, with one person being diagnosed every thirty minutes. In

2025, we lost one Australian to melanoma every six hours. That's someone's partner, parent, sibling, mate, gone. And melanoma doesn't hit everyone the same. I mentioned before that melanoma is the leading cancer in Aussies aged twenty to thirty-nine. It also affects young women more than young men, but once men hit fifty, the risk for them skyrockets. Part of that is because men tend to be worse at checking their skin for changes, worse at wearing sunscreen, worse at going to the doctor when something looks off.

But there's a lot of hope. The science is getting better, and advancements in treatments and early detection have increased survival rates, meaning much better odds for the thousands of Australians facing this disease. The Australian Skin Cancer Foundation will keep funding and supporting new research and life-saving therapies. These medical advances are changing what once felt like a grim diagnosis, offering far more hopeful outcomes.

The future isn't written yet, but it's looking better than it did ten, twenty years ago. And that's something. We've got the tools, we've got the facts and we've got the fight. Survivors are telling their stories, like this one you're reading right now. Schools are teaching kids about hats and sunscreen from day one. And people are listening.

My story is just one of many, but the lesson is universal: awareness and action can save lives. Had I ignored Janine's worries or brushed off those early warning signs, the outcome could have been vastly different for me. Melanoma doesn't discriminate. Melanoma doesn't care about your age, your fitness level or your plans for the future. That's why education, regular skin checks and listening to your body are so critical.

There's a collective feeling of hope in Australia's fight against melanoma. New breakthroughs, like immunotherapy and targeted treatments, are giving patients a second chance. Trials are underway for therapies that could one day become cures. And, perhaps most importantly, there's a growing movement to ensure no-one faces this journey alone.

For me, surviving melanoma wasn't just about beating cancer; it was about gaining a second chance at life and using it well. I believe we're working toward a future where fewer Australians will have to endure this battle, where prevention and early intervention will become the norm, and where melanoma could one day be cured. But for now, I'll keep sharing my story. I want to remind others that their health is worth fighting for, because if my journey has taught me anything, it's that hope and resilience are just as powerful as treatment.

The thing that's kept me going is turning my fear into purpose. I'm so proud that the charity I launched, the Australian Skin Cancer Foundation, now works alongside heavy-hitters like MIA and the Cancer Council. Our goal is simple: spread awareness, not just about treatment, but about prevention.

Australia's UV levels are some of the highest in the world. We're known as the skin cancer capital. And it's not just beach bums and surfers who are at risk – anyone who grew up under this sun could be in trouble. These days, 'melanoma' is a word just about every Aussie knows. It's in our ads, our classrooms, our family stories. And the thing is, so much of it is preventable. When we know better, we can do better. That's what drives me to this day. Most skin cancers are completely avoidable if you slip, slop, slap, seek shade and slide on your sunnies.

I visit schools, building sites, workplaces, wherever I can share my experience. I explain how chasing a tan nearly cost me everything. And I tell people straight: solariums and your skin are a terrible bargain. The confusion, regret, relief – it all becomes real when I say it out loud.

But I always say – melanoma might've knocked me down, but it didn't knock me out. If sharing my story saves even one life, it's worth it. Because this isn't just a battle to survive anymore for me. It's my purpose. Melanoma might have left a few scars, but it's not going to have the last word. I am.

•

Today, I'm fit and healthy. My skin is protected, and my family keep me grounded and happy. It means so much to me that my kids are proud of the work I do with the foundation, too, wanting to wear our t-shirts and help out when they can. Jaxon comes on all the big melanoma walks with me, helping lead the road crews like a trooper. I know deep down that one day he'll run the foundation himself. He's got the right heart, the right head, and he's a tremendous young man. Charli's just the same, quiet strength, full of empathy. I know they'll step up when the time comes. Chloe, Josie and Jayden might all play a major part in the charity one day, too, and Shaylee is so supportive as well, being involved in all the walks and staying connected and supportive on social media to cheer me and the charity on. I couldn't be prouder of all my kids.

What I look forward to most these days are the little things: sunrise dog walks, driving my kids to school, sitting around the dinner table together each day, listening to my wife (who, I've worked out, is always right) and regular gym sessions – strictly for fitness these days, not vanity. What I know now is that true confidence doesn't come from bronzed skin; it comes from knowing you're healthy, and doing everything you can to stay that way.

Most of all, I'm grateful. For second chances. For science. For the people behind sun-smart campaigns, for the researchers in labs all around the world, for every health professional who didn't give up on me and for the incredible, brave people I've met along the way. I've been lashed by UV lights, CT scanners and some pretty brutal treatments, but I'm still here. I'm still standing.

And I'm loving the life I fought for. Eating chips on the beach, sunhat and sunnies firmly in place and a good hit of sunscreen every two hours. I plan on sticking around, long enough to collect more stories worth telling, for my kids and for every Aussie kid whose dreams are golden, but whose future deserves more than a tan.

21

A FINAL THANK YOU

I can't finish this book without shining a light on some of the incredible people I've met along the way, who inspire me every day. Too many of them aren't with us anymore but they are always in my thoughts. Their strength, wisdom and generosity continue to guide everything I do.

I met so many dear mates at that first melanoma-specific support group at the San Hospital. That meeting changed everything.

I met the kind Corinne Leslie, who had lost her dad to melanoma. Judy Middlebrook, an amazing human and a multiple-time survivor herself, was there that day, too.

She invited our family to stay at her property in Canberra many times over the years. Her home was like a retreat. Everything we ate came from her garden, and she was so kind to us. Janine was there at the first meeting with me, and she became close with everyone, too. We were all in it together.

Belinda Selig was there with her husband, Pete, who sadly lost his fight. But Belinda and her family still support everything I do to this day. Judy Mulcahy was also at that first meeting. She passed away not long after I met her, just months after giving birth. She was the first real mate from the support groups I lost to melanoma, and losing her devastated me.

I'll never forget the support from Herman at Melanoma Patients Australia – he helped me through it all. A total legend who taught me how to handle the tough stuff and keep going.

After we started running awareness campaigns and getting more attention in the media, people from all over Australia – and even the UK and US – began reaching out to me. I replied to every message. I knew what it felt like to go through this without support.

I remember Ian Whitmore, a survivor who had no support in Australia. Janine and I visited him in North Sydney and took him for a drive along the coast. We stopped for a pie, his favourite. That was really our first experience of offering one-on-one support. Ian was a champion, but seeing what he was going through was so tough. Before he passed, he said to me (excuse the language), 'Jay, you don't want to get advanced melanoma. The pain is unbearable. Fuck that. It's no way to die.' Those words haunted me for a long time.

Then there was Ian Brown. He was a living legend. We became great mates, helping each other through the fear. His melanoma returned, sadly. When Ian needed a scan to determine his treatment path and couldn't afford it, I paid for it without hesitation. How could I not? I miss him terribly. Before he passed, he told me he'd come back as a blowfly. And I swear, whenever I'm out doing skin checks in the truck, there's always a blowfly buzzing around that doesn't leave. I know it's him.

Brian Snelling, a chef from New Zealand with stage 4 melanoma, was like a brother to me. Our support group would meet then head to our favourite Thai restaurant in Newtown. That place became sacred to us. Every time Janine and I went to RPA for scans, we'd eat there: chilli basil stir-fry and rice. I really believed those meals, full of veggies, were helping keep my immune system strong.

Brian and I became the best of mates. We talked about everything. He'd tell me stories about going on blind dates, always looking for the right woman but never quite finding her. He was an amazing cook, too. I remember he came to our house once to teach Janine and me how to make steak and veggies his 'Kiwi magic' way, and he made us the most magnificent lunch.

When he passed away, it was sudden. I'd caught up with him just days before, for a coffee and a green tea in the city. He was coughing a bit, his voice was rough, but he told me he was fine. The next day, he texted to say he was in hospital with an infection and would be out in a few days. When I went to visit, his family met me at the door and told me the news that Brian had passed. He didn't want me to see him sick or know he was struggling. That was just who he was, thinking of others, even at the end.

It took me a long time to come to terms with losing Brian. At his service, his family asked me to speak. It was an open casket, and I remember standing there, talking to him, wishing I hadn't looked because it wasn't the Brian I knew. But I spoke proudly about our friendship to his family, to our support group mates and to anyone who would listen. I cried my eyes out that day.

Back then, it felt like every month I was losing another friend to melanoma. I remember thinking, *When's my turn?* But that thought only made me more determined to make the most of each day and to keep living and fighting to make sure my mates didn't die in vain.

During this time, I met Carrine Weston, a beautiful human who was fighting melanoma while still doing so much advocacy work. She even held a fundraising night in the Illawarra as she underwent treatment. We started a support group in the region, and Carrine's family, her sister Tennille Shelley and brother-in-law Aaron, let us use their truck office to run the meetings. I remember one time I was asked by the Cancer Institute NSW if I knew anyone with melanoma who might be keen to appear in a summer TV campaign. Carrine put her hand up after much convincing from me. We drove together to the Institute, where she met the team and began preparing to film.

Very sadly, not long after, Carrine developed a tumour in her brain and could no longer participate in the campaign. I'll never forget a barbecue we held for the support group down in Kiama. Carrine was there with her family, but she had a seizure. It was incredibly frightening for everyone, especially her family. To this day, every time I drive past Kiama or see a road sign for it, I think of that afternoon.

Carrine passed away not long after. Her funeral was massive. Tennille and Aaron Shelley have supported every-thing I've done since. They're grateful for the friendship I had with Carrine, and they are some of the kindest, most generous people I know. I remember when we held a fundraising concert with Shannon Noll in the Illawarra and barely broke even, but Aaron wouldn't have it. He quietly chipped in around $25,000 to make sure we made a profit. He's a living legend who helps families and people behind the scenes and never asks for credit. He just does it because it's the right thing to do.

Even now, he'll send fuel cards to help keep the Skin Check Truck on the road or lend a hand whenever it's needed. He and Tennille are good people, like family to me. They're also very private and probably wouldn't want me writing this, but sometimes credit is deserved.

That same night of the fundraising concert, Shannon Noll kindly jumped in my car during a break in the show. We drove a few kilometres to the hospital in Kiama to visit a young man called Glen Lawrence, who was in palliative care with melanoma. It was his birthday, and Shannon sang 'Happy Birthday' to him right there in his room. Then we jumped back in the car and returned to the concert. Glen was over the moon. It meant the world to him. He passed not long after, but his family still remembers that moment.

I was lucky to meet Katie-Lee Spence, a young mum who held a fundraising dinner in Townsville. She was very sick at the time and *60 Minutes* was preparing to do a story about her, focused on her decision to stop the treatment she was meant to be on. Sadly, she passed away before the story could be filmed. I'm still great mates with her best friend Briohny and her mum, Debi Spence.

And then there was Dennis Inggs, who had written a heartfelt letter to 2GB's Ray Hadley saying he had been given a melanoma death sentence and asking Ray to look out for his family. I got to know Dennis well, and we became good mates. I brought him along to our support groups, and he was such a strong young man. One time, we all went to the NRL State of Origin together, and Ray had organised for Dennis to get a behind-the-scenes tour of the New South Wales team's sheds. When Dennis passed away, Ray stepped in again. He helped have the family home in rural New South Wales renovated and arranged financial support for them. Such a kind thing to do. Since then, I've become great friends with Dennis's mum, Alex, and his sister, Janine. They're beautiful people who've supported me at so many events over the years.

It was during this time that Nicole Gillespie entered my life. As I mentioned, we organised for Nicole to meet the Queensland State of Origin team – this was the same night Dennis was there. Queensland won the series, and Nicole even got to go out onto the field after the game to help lift the Origin shield. It was such a special moment, and I'm just glad we were able to tee that up for her. She absolutely loved it.

Nicole later invited me to go to the Logies with her. I remember how excited she was – she knew everyone's names, especially the cast of *Home and Away*, and got me to take photos with her camera (this was before iPhones) of almost every famous person we saw. I gladly played photographer for her the whole night.

She was very sick at the time, with visible tumours, but that didn't stop her from having the time of her life. Six weeks later, Nicole passed away.

Amanda Zoratto was married to a family friend of ours, Craig Higbid. Craig called me out of the blue one day and said, 'Jay, I need your help. My wife has stage 4 melanoma.' Amanda and I also became great mates. She was a beautiful human who desperately wanted to live. She didn't want to leave behind her young family. Sadly, Amanda passed away not long after, in 2015. Craig was (and still is) a champion human. A gentle soul who, years later, would support me through my own cancer treatment in 2021.

There was Ken 'The Foo Fighter', a strong, inspiring human who loved the Foo Fighters so much, he even started a campaign to meet the band. I still remember visiting him in hospital toward the end. He was as strong as an ox, but this cruel disease eventually got him. His wife, Ann, and daughter, Tara, are beautiful humans who continue to help the foundation at every opportunity. They're incredibly loyal and always do what they can in honour of their Ken.

I also met Maura Luxford in the very early days. She had lost her daughter Hannah to melanoma when Hannah was just twenty years old. Maura went on to write a book called *ride4acure*, and in one of the most powerful awareness campaigns I've ever seen, she rode a horse across Australia in memory of Hannah. My family and I are still great mates with Maura. Even now, we continue to support each other through various events. Her strength inspires me every day.

A story of my life wouldn't be complete without mentioning Nathan Jones, a bloody champion. A smart guy, a schoolteacher and the one who started the Melanoma March in Melbourne. He also ran support groups and became one of my closest mates for many years.

This is where Ruth Davey's story comes in. Her husband, Rob, called me one day in a panic. He said, 'Jay, you've got to do something. They've told Ruth she needs treatment for melanoma but it's going to cost several hundred thousand dollars. We just don't have that kind of money.' I told him to leave it with me.

Here's where it gets wild. Just a few days later, Nathan called me one Saturday morning and said, 'Jay, you're not going to believe this. Ron Walker, the chairman of the Australian Grand Prix, is sitting opposite me at a cafe.' I knew Ron had beaten stage 4 melanoma, so I told Nathan, 'Mate, we need his help. Go get his business card.'

Nathan went up to him, told him his own story and Ruth's, and Ron asked that Rob reach out to his assistant. I immediately rang Rob and said, 'Mate, you won't believe it, but Ron might be able to help.' Rob emailed as instructed, and a few weeks later, Ruth and Rob were called into their oncologist's office. The oncologist said, 'I don't know what you've done, but you're starting treatment next week . . . no charge.'

It was magic. The treatment worked, and Ruth is still here today to tell the story.

I've since become great mates with Ruth, Rob and their whole family. Ruth actually looks so much like Olivia Newton-John that one day I reached out to Olivia's manager and organised for Ruth to meet her as a surprise, before her concert with John Farnham in Sydney. It was a special moment where Ruth got to meet her twin. Olivia even arranged front-row seats for us, and after the show, we found ourselves backstage having a glass of wine with

Olivia, John, his manager Glenn Wheatley and the crew. A night none of us will ever forget.

There was Astley Friend, just twenty-four years old, a brilliant young man studying science. He used to drive up to our Central Coast melanoma support meetings once a month on a Saturday. I'll never forget the day James and I visited him in Westmead Hospital during his final days. He was incredibly sick but still managed to thank us for being there. My last memory of Astley is of him coughing as we left his palliative care room. Every time I pass a sign for Westmead Hospital, I think of him. Ian Brown died there, too. And it's also where I had my own interferon treatment back in 2008. That place holds a lot.

Rachel Richards was another close mate who passed away in 2013. I remember going with her to an appointment in Manly. She'd done a huge amount of research into alternative treatments and was determined to try anything that might help. Sadly, her melanoma spread to her brain. She was an integral part of our Central Coast support group, and her passing came as a huge shock to all of us.

Then there's Jenny Thulborn, a warrior and a dear friend. Jenny and I are still close today. I used to pick her up from the airport and drive her to her appointments. She's had more than eight tumours in her brain, not to mention melanoma in various parts of her body, but thanks to world-leading melanoma doctors and the latest treatments, she's still here. One of the highlights for her was visiting the set of *The Today Show*, where she got to meet all the stars of morning TV. She's never forgotten it.

There was also Ruby, who became a great friend of mine. We supported each other through our melanoma battles, leaning on each other when we needed strength. Ruby had it incredibly tough. I remember visiting her in palliative care in Brisbane with our mutual friend and fellow survivor Louise. Ruby was asleep when we arrived, but when she stirred and saw us, she smiled and called me 'Superman'. Her last words to me were, 'Never stop, my Superman.' Every time I see her beautiful face on the 'In Memory' board of our Skin Check Truck, I hear them again.

Louise, who was with me that day, is another incredible person. We first met in 2013 at a cafe in Sydney when she was going through treatment for a tumour in her liver. Thanks to immunotherapy, she's still clear to this day. She's a bright light, incredibly smart and someone I continue to lean on for advice and perspective. A truly switched-on human and a dear mate.

The De Young family from Melbourne have also been amazing supporters of everything I do. They lost their beloved Scott to melanoma in 2014. He was just thirty-five years old. Scott's story gained national attention as he raised significant funds to access treatment. His brother Ben is a champion bloke and has supported several of our melanoma walks. Their ongoing support means the world.

The team at the Rollonin Cafe in Bowning, New South Wales, have become like family to me, too. That's one of the beautiful things to come out of my battle with melanoma – I have a very large extended family now! The owner, Tony Ryan, was diagnosed with melanoma and, even while undergoing treatment, finished building the cafe. An absolute legend. Renata and the rest of the family have supported every melanoma walk we've done, showing up with heart and generosity every time. They're just good people through and through.

I met Laurie Thompson in 2015 after he was diagnosed with stage 3 melanoma. A top bloke, Laurie and I became great mates, often attending support groups together. After beating melanoma, he had a seizure one night and was rushed to hospital. James and I visited him soon after. A few days later, Laurie was diagnosed with an aggressive form of brain cancer. He asked me to join him for his first appointment. His entire family was in the room when the doctor gave him the grim diagnosis of just fifteen to eighteen months to live. His mum dropped to the floor crying, his sister broke down in tears, but Laurie, always tough, walked out of the room and said, 'Oh well, I'll be okay.' He was stoic until the end, passing away at just thirty-five.

It was at a fundraiser for Laurie that James and I noticed a young woman with a suspicious mole on her arm. We approached her and asked if she'd had it checked. She hadn't, but James told her the story of his son, Michael, who had passed away from melanoma. That following Monday, I booked her in at the Mawson Skin Cancer Clinic in Campbelltown. The mole was removed and it turned out to be melanoma. Catching it early likely saved her life. That night was fate at its best.

There was also Jack, a local painter who came to quote for painting my house. As he walked back to his car, I noticed a dark mole on the back of his neck. I asked if he'd had it checked – he said his GP had looked at it and thought it was fine. I told him it didn't look right and that I'd be more comfortable if he had it biopsied. I booked him in the next day in Bowral. The results came back – melanoma. Thankfully, it hadn't spread to his lymph nodes. Jack later told me his GP had removed the same mole five years earlier with a shave biopsy, but not all the cells were taken out, which is how it came back. Now, he jokes that I've got a lifetime of free painting.

Gaby Rogers from Channel 9 has been a huge mentor and supporter over the years. She's been part of my journey since my diagnosis in 2008, covering my story in countless segments and giving me tips and feedback on how to work with the media and politicians. Gaby even came to my five-year cancer-free celebration. I have huge respect for her – she's an amazing human and a great journalist.

Ash Piek is another incredible woman. She lost her mum to melanoma in 2021. Ash first reached out to me when her mum was given bad news and was searching for treatment options, and I connected her with Professor Grant McArthur AO in Melbourne. Ash has been by my side ever since, helping to guide where the Australian Skin Cancer Foundation is today. We wouldn't be where we are without her.

We've also been fortunate to receive support from some amazing sponsors and businesses. Toyota, and especially Ally and the team there, have been unwavering in their support. Project Dry Hire's Aaron and Tennille Shelley never stop – they've stood by me for years. Steve Grant from Street Impact has done all the branding for our Toyota support cars for free and continues to mentor me. He's a true friend.

I'm also incredibly grateful to Ron and the team at Ricky Richards for everything they do to back our work.

There's also Jason Laurie from Cement Australia – this guy is a legend, as I mentioned earlier. Without him, we wouldn't have the Skin Check Truck on the road.

I can't forget Hayley Bourke, a beautiful soul who became a dear friend. Despite being given just six weeks to live, she insisted on leading our 2022 melanoma walk, pushed in a wheelchair at both the start and finish lines. Before she passed, Hayley quietly told me she was leaving money in her will to help launch our Skin Check Truck. I'll never forget that moment. Her husband, Lawrence Polga, has kept that promise and now joins us at every walk. He's a true warrior honouring his wife's legacy.

Tas Smethurst and Grant Lawrence are two more mates I'm so grateful to have met. I first met Tas and his wife, Amanda, with Nicole Gillespie during a visit to their tea house in Exeter. We became close friends, even hosting a talk on skin cancer prevention at Chevalier College in Burradoo. When Tas's melanoma advanced and he became too unwell, my family went down to their property, mowing the lawns and helping out wherever we could. Amanda and their girls moved to Taree after Tas passed, and we stayed connected. She's a great friend, and she's always been a huge support for me, too.

Grant, meanwhile, is a miracle. I first met him in his twenties, and he had tumours in his lungs, liver and spine.

The odds were against him, but immunotherapy worked. He's now been clear for around seven years, off treatment and still cheeky as ever. I truly believe he's been cured.

I wouldn't be where I am today without all these beautiful people. There are so many more, and you all know who you are. I keep the people we've lost in my heart, always, and they are honoured on the 'In Memory' wall of the Skin Check Truck. When I finish a day on the road, I turn back and nod at them. I feel them with me every step of the way, guiding me and lifting me up.

There are also the many incredible people who help keep our foundation going.

One of them is stage 4 melanoma survivor Elise Beaton. Through her business, Elka Print & Merchandise, Elise handles all of our branding. It's those directly affected by melanoma who often help keep our truck on the road and our mission alive. Elise had numerous tumours but, thanks to the latest treatments, is now all clear. Tragically, not long after her recovery, Elise and her family lost their twelve-year-old son to brain cancer. Despite this heartbreaking loss, Elise remains at the heart of our work.

Paula Jackson from Port Macquarie is another beautiful human who has been through so much. After losing her sister to melanoma, Paula herself battled and survived stage 4 melanoma. Every time we travel to Queensland, we stop in Port Macquarie, and Paula always welcomes us with open arms, offering us a place to stay, storing the truck and helping us get back on the road bright and early.

I have to thank Raphael McGowan, the founder of Bakslap, who's a legend of a human. We've been mates since 2012. Katrina Parks is another beautiful human and a survivor. Another great mate of mine is Katie Hook, who lost her dad to melanoma. And whenever I venture to the Gold Coast, I always train with Luke Hayes, who lost his dad to melanoma. It's a 5 am session and you know it's going to be tough, but it's a great bunch of old NRL players with plenty of banter.

My mate Kyle Horro, a stage 4 melanoma survivor, is another champion. We meet every few months to talk about life and what we've been through. Renee Darling is another dear friend and a fellow survivor. There's also Louise Farmer, who I met ten years ago when I was having an event in Bathurst. She walked past and recognised me, and we've been great mates ever since. Jody and Dion have been great mates of mine, too. Jody was diagnosed with stage 3 melanoma after I was. Together, we have conquered our fears. I love these guys.

I'm forever thankful to our ambassadors, including Australian cricket great Michael Clarke and the NRL's Braith Anasta. They are all absolute legends. And I cannot forget Deb Knight, who has been unbelievably supportive of all we do. It was Deb and a segment on Channel 9's *A Current Affair* that got the attention of Jason Laurie and his wife, and helped us get our first Skin Check Truck.

I need to thank a PR company called Kit Communications, too. The director, Deahne Hemphill, is an amazing human who has also been affected by melanoma. Kit Communications have supported all I do for years now, including our 2000-kilometre fifty-day melanoma walk in 2019. The PR they secured for us broke records, just like the walk.

Finally, Maria Totorica also became a dear friend after she lost her 21-year-old daughter, Kali, to melanoma. Maria often says that having Kali's photo featured on the side of our Skin Check Truck helps keep her daughter's memory alive. She finds comfort in watching the truck's journey across the country and knowing that Kali is still out there, making a difference. It means the world to her, and it means the world to me, too. People often stop in front of the truck to cry, to take photos, to remember. Some drive by and film us from their cars. I know they're grieving as well. They're seeing someone they love on the side of that truck, and if that helps in some small way – if it brings a moment of pride, a bit of peace or even a smile – then I know we're doing the right thing. We've had people tell us their loved one is now seeing more of the country than they ever did in their life.

People often ask how I keep going – how I do what I do. But I don't stop long enough to think about it. I just do it. Because I've met the most extraordinary humans in the fight of their lives. I carry them with me, and I like to think they're proud of what we've built.

They're the real heroes.

They're the reason we're still rolling.

They're the reason lives are being saved.

POSTSCRIPT

The strange thing about telling your story is that it forces you to look back and remember all the good, the bad and everything in between. It's surreal, in a way. But more than anything, it makes you realise how lucky you are for the people you've met along the way.

I've always hoped that what I was doing was making a difference. That all the walking, talking, sharing and campaigning meant something. And sometimes, the biggest reminder of that comes from the people who walked beside me. They're the ones who saw it all up close.

So I wanted to include a few of their voices here. These are the words of a handful of the amazing people who played a part in this journey: mates, supporters, professionals and advocates. It's a strange thing to read about yourself like this, but it's also a privilege. Because at the end of the day, for me, it's always just been about saving lives.

> In 2010, melanoma survivor Jay Allen came to see me for help in having commercial solaria banned. I introduced him to the politician Frank Sartor AO. Together, Jay and Frank were like public health bull terriers on a bone, and New South Wales banned these melanoma incubators from January 2015. Other states then followed. Jay is a public health hero whose passionate ongoing educational work is simply majestic.
>
> PROFESSOR SIMON CHAPMAN AO, Emeritus Professor in Public Health at the University of Sydney

> I first met Jay not long after his surgery. From memory, he had already been on television speaking about his melanoma diagnosis and treatment. He was referred to me for general support and adjustment. Before sharing anything about our work together, I gave this a great deal

of thought and only agreed after Jay himself asked if I would share some insights – and once both he and Janine had given their full consent.

When I think back to those early sessions, what I remember most vividly was how young he was – a young man who was terrified, numb, anxious and overwhelmed all at once, trying to process what it meant to be diagnosed with such a serious and aggressive cancer. His diagnosis was not only a threat to his life, but also to his sense of self – it shook his certainty about where life was headed, his identity as a fit, strong young man, a husband, and someone who had always taken pride in his health and physicality. Alongside this was the impact of surgery – both functionally and aesthetically – and the quiet, painful question of how Janine would see him now. Would she still find him attractive? Would others see him differently? These were raw, deeply human fears that touched on the very essence of who he was.

So much had happened in such a short space of time: a frightening diagnosis, major surgery, marrying his partner and suddenly finding himself a public figure. Yet somehow, through the fear and uncertainty, Jay found courage. Even then, in those early days, he began using his voice to advocate, to raise awareness and to build what would become a powerful movement for change.

Jay has always been a 'what you see is what you get' kind of person. In the beginning, he struggled with self-confidence – not self-belief, because he always believed in the cause – but sometimes the confidence to recognise his own worth and potential. He'd often say, 'I'm just a truck driver; I do my job and go to the gym – now I can't even go back to that.' Yet despite the fear, the loss and the self-doubt, he kept showing up. He balanced supporting other patients, advocating for awareness and research, and coming to counselling to do the difficult work of unpacking what he was living through. There were dark and painful times, but Jay found strength in vulnerability, and within that, a remarkable ability to make meaning of his experience and to grow through it.

He and Janine, at different times, came to counselling together, navigating the fears and pressures that come with such an enormous life change. It didn't take long to realise that Janine was his superpower – her love, patience and support gave Jay the steadiness he needed to keep giving so much of himself to others. Together, they faced the hard parts head-on, showing enormous courage, love and determination to find their way through.

Life has thrown Jay several curveballs that have undoubtedly left their mark. He bears not only the physical scars but also the emotional and psychological ones – and those deeper wounds still show themselves from time to time. What helps Jay manage them is his ongoing willingness to show up and check in when he needs to talk things through – something I deeply admire, especially given how much support he provides to others. Jay is a husband, a father, a friend and a person whom literally hundreds of people rely on for guidance, encouragement and hope. He has somehow turned his voice into something that creates enormous good – transforming ideas into actions, and actions into tangible, accessible services that reach entire communities.

He has learned how to lean into his experience, his trauma and his story to get him to where he wants to be and how he wants to be. He has worked hard by coming to and seeking counselling and doing what has often been difficult work in therapy – to be open, to unpack the hard things, and to learn ways to manage and enhance his psychological and emotional resilience and wellbeing. I am in awe of his strength, his ability to foster community, create change, and perhaps most of all, his ability to connect to people and lean into his very human feelings and experiences.

ANGELA, Counsellor

I've known Jay Allen since 2018, when I joined him for The Longest Melanoma March – a casual little stroll from Brisbane to Sydney (only 1200 kilometres or so!) to raise awareness and funds for melanoma research. From the very first day I met him, it was clear that Jay isn't just passionate about melanoma awareness – he lives and breathes it. Whether it's chatting to locals at a rest stop or speaking to a packed community hall, Jay has an incredible knack for connecting with people and turning every conversation into an opportunity to educate, support and inspire.

I originally met Jay in a professional capacity – filming a documentary about his walk – but it didn't take long for that working relationship to transform into a genuine friendship. Since then, we've become good mates, teaming up to share his story and message with an even wider audience. Through film, social media and community events, it's been incredibly rewarding to help amplify the impact of what Jay started on those long, hot roads.

While I haven't been personally affected by melanoma, Jay has shown me how deeply it impacts so many lives. He's relentless in his mission to make sure no-one faces it alone – connecting patients and families with local support networks, sharing stories and offering encouragement that feels as genuine as it gets.

In 2019, I joined Jay again on another of his 'short walks' – this time, a 2000-kilometre trek from Adelaide to Sydney. Across countless blisters, busted shoes and stretches of endless road, I watched Jay walk side by side with people whose lives had been changed by melanoma. He listened, laughed, cried and carried their stories with him every step of the way. No matter how tough the conditions got, his compassion and humour never wavered – and somehow, he always managed to make everyone else feel stronger, even when he was the one hobbling.

Jay's energy is infectious, his heart is enormous, and his dedication is unmatched. He's the kind of person who reminds you that one person really can make a difference – even if it means wearing out a few dozen pairs of shoes along the way.

JOHN BENSLEY, Cameraman

Friendships are built on many different foundations. The first day I saw Jay Allen's name was on the wall of the waiting room in RPA's Cancer Centre. It was on a scrappy bit of paper that said 'Call this number to join a support group'.

I thought to myself, *I wonder who this Jay Allen is?* I didn't call the number! Life took over. I had a five-week-old baby, and I was twelve weeks post-operation having my melanoma removed.

Fast forward from that moment in the late 2000s to now. Jay Allen is my friend, my colleague in trying to make sure every Australian has access to free, high-quality skin cancer checks, and a survivor of not one but two life-threatening cancers.

We laugh a lot! We have shared moments that most friends don't – we've cried when the physical pain has got too much, we tell each other the truth (not what we want to hear but need to hear), and when we don't answer each other's phone calls, we are intensely disappointed in one another!

I admire his ability to push and to see the YES in everything even if it sounds impossible. Jay, you've achieved so much since I saw your name and number on that wall – as a husband, a dad, a friend, a dragon of breathing dreams to life.

Your energy, passion and focus are extreme. You are extreme, and you are loved by an extreme number of people who owe so much to you and your dreams.

JANE MAHONY, Melanoma Survivor

 The first time I met Jay in 2008, he was known as The Melanoma Man and had featured on Channel 9's *RPA* program, having undergone treatment for his cancer. What struck me most about Jay was not only his dedication to his family, in light of a life-threatening diagnosis, but his determination to ensure no other family had to face the same predicament.

I admire Jay's tenacity in successfully lobbying governments, here and overseas, to ban cancer-causing solariums. He galvanised an army of supporters, both at a grassroots and government level, to make it happen. Jay is a real doer and turns his vision into reality, as seen with the Australian Skin Cancer Foundation and the mobile skin cancer check truck. On top of that, he has always had a strong understanding of the media, with a natural ability to sense what makes a compelling story, and has generously given me numerous interviews over the years.

Jay is always humble and compassionate; I'm very proud to call him my friend. It takes courage and empathy to draw from your own experience fighting cancer and turn that into meaningful change, improving the lives of others.

GABY ROGERS, Channel 9 Health Reporter

 We first met Jay Allen around 2009, during one of the hardest times our family has ever faced. Tennille's sister Carrine was battling melanoma, and Jay was there offering compassion, understanding and genuine support. His kindness and empathy made an enormous difference – not only to her but to all of us.

Since then, Jay has never stopped fighting. He has devoted his life to helping others, raising awareness and driving meaningful change in the fight against skin cancer. What stands out most about Jay is his heart. He wears it proudly on his sleeve – open, honest and full of passion for every person he meets. He has a rare ability to lift others even in their darkest moments, and his enthusiasm for finding a cure and supporting those affected by this terrible disease is truly inspiring.

We have the deepest respect for Jay – not just as a leader and advocate, but as a friend and a remarkable human being. His achievements, particularly establishing the Australian Skin Cancer Foundation and getting two mobile Skin Check Trucks on the road, are nothing short of extraordinary. Many would have seen that goal as impossible. Jay may not have known exactly how to begin, but he had the courage to try – and he made it happen.

We're so proud of everything he's accomplished and the countless lives he's touched along the way. Jay, we love you, we thank you, and we're forever grateful for everything you've done – and continue to do – for so many.

AARON and TENNILLE SHELLEY

We met Jay back in 2011. He greeted us with a huge smile and wonderful energy. We remember him saying to us, 'If you ever need me to help in any way, please call me.' Well, we have made thousands of calls to this amazing man over time and never has he ever let us down, getting us through our journey with skin cancer, from finding out Ruth had less than twelve months to live over ten years ago to where we are today.

Jay got us through the toughest of times – day and night, coming into the hospitals, crying with us and holding our hands when the news wasn't good. He's truly an Australian hero. He helps so many people and has nothing but pure kindness in his big heart. We owe Ruth's life to him, and we're eternally grateful to him for helping us reach our dreams of getting clear results. We love him and he deserves the world. Cheers to a champion!

RUTH and ROB DAVEY

My friendship with Jay Allen, founder of the Australian Skin Cancer Foundation, is something I hold very close to my heart. Jay was an incredible source of strength and support during my late wife Melinda ('M') Beaumont's courageous battle with melanoma while under the exceptional care of the Melanoma Institute Australia. Alongside Jay, James Economides was also a pillar of support during that heartbreaking time, and I will be forever grateful for their compassion, kindness and unwavering presence when it mattered most.

Since then, Jay has continued to dedicate himself tirelessly to the fight against melanoma, raising awareness, driving education and championing early detection through skin checks and advocacy. His passion for this cause is extraordinary and deeply inspiring. Over the years, I've had the privilege of joining Jay on several of his charity walks, including last year's unforgettable full-time walk from Canberra to Sydney via Batemans Bay and along the stunning South Coast of NSW. The camaraderie, determination and shared mission to conquer this devastating disease created a sense of unity and hope that I will never forget. Beyond the walks, we've worked together to raise awareness through initiatives at my son's school, The Scots College, hosting the Skin Check Truck and encouraging students to spread the word about early-detection efforts that have already led to life-saving interventions.

I cannot speak highly enough of Jay's commitment and the unwavering support of his family. His relentless drive to push for greater awareness, research and political action is nothing short of remarkable. I am proud to call Jay and the incredible friends I've gained through this journey my allies in the fight against melanoma. Together, we honour M's memory and work toward a future where this disease no longer claims lives.

DEAN BEAUMONT

The first photo is of me on my final day of treatment in 2021, just seventy kilos, drained and barely standing. The second is me in 2022, eighty-eight kilos, stronger than I'd felt in a long time and now the CEO of the Australian Skin Cancer Foundation. I wanted to share these photos to give hope and show that you can recover, and things can get better. I know that's not the case for everyone, but early detection is key.

ACKNOWLEDGEMENTS

To my wife, Janine – you are the soul of my survival. Through every cancer battle, every fear, every night when I wasn't sure I could face another day, you stood there. You listened to thousands of recaps of this journey, the highs and the heartbreaks. You kept our family standing when I couldn't stand myself. You moved through chaos with a calm that still amazes me – nothing fazes you, not even the storms that tore through our lives. You think it's nothing because you're humble, but to me, it is everything. I love you more than these pages can hold, and I am grateful for you with every breath I breathe.

To my beautiful mum – my first protector, my first believer. When cancer tried to break me, your words built me back up: 'You'll be right, son. I have a good feeling you'll be okay.' You said it with love, with certainty, with a mother's faith that could defeat anything. Those words carried me when I was too weak to carry myself. You have been there every second of my life – loving me, guiding me, every scan, every fear, making sure I never went without, not food, not love, not hope. I love you, Mum. Thank you for being my anchor when the world felt like it was disappearing under my feet.

To my dad – thank you for every training run, every footy conversation, every moment you backed my dreams. Love you, mate.

To my children – you are the reason I fought. You are the reason I'm still here.

Jaxon – my strong-willed, big-hearted son. You care for others in ways that show real strength. Don't ever doubt what you're capable of. I see leadership in you – I see a future where you're running the Australian Skin Cancer Foundation. Chase those footy dreams, son. Be patient. Your moment will come. Love you lots!

Charli – love you so much, Charli girl. You have a fire inside you, on the footy field and in life. When things get hard, keep pushing. Keep tackling, keep passing, keep kicking, keep setting up tries – not just for the team, but for yourself. You are unstoppable in all forms of life, so never doubt yourself, and believe in who you are.

Chloe – my beautiful girl. You shine in ways that are impossible to miss. Your dreams – footy, singing, every spark inside you – are yours to chase with everything you have. Never doubt your confidence. It's one of your greatest gifts. I love you endlessly.

Josie girl – believe in yourself always. You can conquer anything, because you have a strength in you that the world hasn't fully seen yet. Follow your siblings, learn from them and then climb even higher. I love you, beautiful baby girl.

Shaylee – I love you. You have been a great support for me and your brothers and sisters. And participating in all the melanoma walks and FaceTiming me all the time, especially when I was sick in 2021, just shows you have a heart of gold. It is hard when we live in different states, but I am so proud of the way you work nonstop and are so focused on your family. You are self-driven and I know your nursing dream is waiting for you when you are ready. You are a beautiful soul and I am so proud of the woman you have grown into.

Jayden – I'm sorry life has pulled us apart at times. But never doubt this: I love you, son. Always.

To my sister Chantal – thank you for your support, your presence, your heart. I love you deeply.

To my sister Shauna – you're not here, but your spirit is with us in every victory, every step forward. I know you're proud. One day, I'll see you again. Love you always.

To James Economides – your support and mentorship has never wavered, my brother. We know that Michael is helping from above and is proud of the human you are and everything you continue to achieve. Love you, mate!

To my mother-in-law Chris, sister-in-law Jaclyn, brother-in-law John and father-in-law John – thank you. Love you guys.

To Kelly Gaudry – thank you for pushing me, for believing in me and for helping this book become real.

To every volunteer, every donor and every person who walked beside us during the melanoma walks – my heart thanks you. We could not have done a single kilometre without your strength and compassion. Your footsteps helped carry us forward – every walk, every time.

To Vanessa and the team at Hachette – thank you for guiding me through this process with patience and belief.

To Scott Henderson – thank you for helping weave my journey into these pages, and for helping shape my pain and my hope into something that can reach others.

To my team at the Australian Skin Cancer Foundation – Sally Everett, Eve Brown, Ash Piek and the whole team – thank you for believing in me, for pushing me, for keeping me focused on the mission when life tries to drag me back. You give me courage, you give me direction, you give me purpose.

And finally – to my mates who lost their lives to melanoma . . . I carry you with me. Every step I take, every word I speak, every life I try to save – you are there. I will never stop fighting for you.

To every family who has lost someone to melanoma or non-melanoma skin cancer – your grief drives this mission. Your stories are the reason I refuse to quit.

Our work isn't done. Not until mobile Skin Check Trucks travel every corner of this country, catching melanoma when it's nothing more than a tiny, tiny lesion. Not until lives stop being stolen by a disease that can be caught early and beaten.

Everything I do is for you. Everything we do is for you. And I won't stop. Not now. Not ever.

For more information about the Australian Skin Cancer Foundation and the mobile Skin Check Trucks, visit australianskincancerfoundation.org.

✉ info@ausskincancer.org

austn australianskincancerfoundation

australianskincancerfoundation